Macromedia®

FLASH 4

Copyright - Editions ENI - May 2000
ISBN: 2-7460-0971-4
Original edition: ISBN: 2-7460-1017-8

ENI Publishing LTD

500 Chiswick High Road
London W4 5RG

Tel: 020 8956 2320
Fax: 020 8956 2321

e-mail: publishing@ediENI.com
http://www.publishing-eni.com

Editions ENI

BP 32125
44021 NANTES Cedex 1

Tel: 33.2.51.80.15.15
Fax: 33.2.51.80.15.16

e-mail: editions@ediENI.com
http://www.editions-eni.com

Straight to the Point collection directed by Corinne HERVO

Foreword

The aim of this book is to help you find rapidly all the features of the **Flash 4** application.

While the examples used are taken from the Windows environment, the commands are the same as those used with a Macinthosh, except for: windows management, some dialog boxes such as Open and Save, and some keys. Below are the corresponding Macintosh keys:

The final pages are given over to an **index** of the topics covered and an **appendix** of Windows and Macintosh shortcut keys.

The typographic conventions used in this book are as follows:

Type faces used for specific purposes:	
bold	indicates the option to take in a menu or dialog box.
italic	is used for notes and comments.
[Ctrl]	represents a key from the keyboard; when two keys appear side by side, they should be pressed simultaneously.

Symbols indicating the content of a paragraph:	
▓	an action to carry out (activating an option, clicking with the mouse...).
⇨	a general comment on the command in question.
⌐🖰	a technique which involves the mouse.
⬡	a keyboard technique.

▣ INTRODUCTION

▣ DRAWING AND GRAPHIC OBJECTS

▣ MOVIE PRINCIPLES

▣ MAKING MOVIES

5⃞ INTERACTIVITY

6⃞ TESTING/PUBLISHING/EXPORTING

APPENDICES

INDEX

Flash 4

1.1 Overview

A-General principles

▓ Macromedia Flash 4 enables you to design simple graphic objects and/or to make complex movies. This application can be used to create complete Web sites using attractive animations with synchronised sound and striking effects, and also animated logos and navigation controls.

▓ The general principle of Flash 4 is about the creation of movies, made using objects you have drawn or imported, and the creation of a stage in which the movie will run according to the Timeline. Flash 4 enables you to make this movie interactive by making it react to events. Once you have tested the movie and are satisfied with it, you can export it as a Flash Player movie, which you can integrate into an HTML page. You can then transfer that page onto the Web server of your choice.

▓ Due to the fact that you can create pictures and Flash movies in the same interface, using drawing tools that are integrated into the software, Flash 4 is a popular application amongst developers. Webmasters also appreciate the fact that pictures and movies created using Flash 4 are very compact, meaning a considerable reduction in the download time of pages containing Flash elements.

▓ Globally, Macromedia Flash 4 can be used to create Web sites with vector or bitmap format graphics, movies, interactive items, forms, and MP3 sounds.

B-Flash Player

▓ From the point of view of the Web user, Flash movies can be interpreted by several platforms, such as Macintosh, Linux and Solaris. But surfers absolutely must have a Flash Player in order to be able to read Web pages that contain Flash elements. This program is supplied with Flash 4, and also with the latest versions of Netscape Communicator and Internet Explorer. As Flash Player is a compact program, you can also download it from www.macromedia.com.

C-Flash 4 characteristics

▓ The graphics created with Macromedia Flash 4 are vector graphics, which explains why Flash animations are so compact, unlike other graphics used on the Web, which are bitmap files (JPG, GIF and PNG). Comparatively, an animated GIF picture uses four times as much disk space as a vector graphic.

▓ Vector graphics are easy to create, and their appearance can be changed by modifying their outline and colours without losing any of the quality of their appearance.

- You cannot create standard bitmap graphics (in JPG, GIF, TIFF etc format) in Flash 4, but you can import them and make modifications such as changing the colours and applying effects. Remember that bitmap graphics are made up of pixels, and that the size of these pixels is defined by the resolution when the graphic is created. Consequently, if you enlarge a bitmap graphic, all you have done is enlarge the size of the pixels, and you do not obtain any more detail.

- Both these types of graphic have their advantages. For example, it would be difficult to convert a digital photograph to a vector graphic format. By the same token, vector graphics are particularly well adapted to laser printers due to their clear outlines, whereas bitmap images become ragged when enlarged.

D-Different Flash 4 movies

There are three main types of movie:

- The **frame-by-frame** principle consists of creating as many pictures as there are graphic steps. By displaying the frames successively, you create an animation effect. This technique has the advantage of producing very precise animations, but has a relatively long download time.

- The **shape tweening** movie principle consists of creating a start picture and an end picture, then automatically interpolating the steps in between. This method is a bit like morphing.

- The third animation principle is **motion tweening**. You create a start picture, define its arrival position and draw its trajectory, which does not have to be in a straight line. The end picture may differ from that at the start in its size, rotation and colour, but it must use the same shape.

1.2 The environment

A-Starting/leaving Macromedia Flash 4

- To start the application in the Windows environment, click the **Start** button, open the **Programs - Macromedia Flash 4** menu, and point to and click **Flash 4**.

- To start the application in the Macintosh environment, double-click the shortcut on the desktop.

- To leave the application, close its window. In the Windows environment:

File	Click the ☒ button on	
Exit	the application window	

B-Description of the workscreen

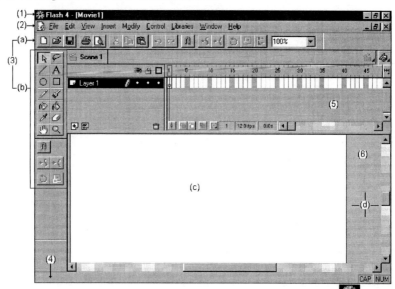

(1) The **title bar** contains the system menu button ![icon], followed by the name of the application and the active movie, as well as buttons that allow you to manage the main Flash 4 window.

(2) The **menu bar** contains the names of the different Flash 4 menus, and, to the right, the ![icon], ![icon] and ![icon] buttons for managing the active movie window.

(3) The **Standard** toolbar (a) contains shortcuts for standard menu commands such as **Open** and **Print**, and the Flash **Drawing** toolbar (b) contains drawing tools and their modifiers.

(4) The **status bar** shows information about the commands and buttons as well as the status of the Caps Lock (CAP) and Num Lock (NUM) keys.

(5) The **Timeline** window allows you to define the different sequences of a movie by coordinating the timing and defining the layering of the graphic objects.

(6) The **workspace** is made up of a workscreen or **stage** (c), which corresponds to the display area of the movie, and is surrounded by a **work area** (d). Objects (or parts of objects) temporarily placed in the work area do not appear in the movie.

C-Using the menus

▤ To open a menu, click its name on the menu bar to see all the available commands. You can also open a menu by pressing `Alt` and the underlined letter in the menu's name. For example, pressing `Alt` **F** will open the **File** menu.

▤ To see a context menu in Windows, click an element to select it, then right-click the selection. In Macintosh, press `⌘ ⌘`nd click.

⇨ *A context menu only displays options that are relative to the current selection.*

D-Showing/hiding the grid and rulers

▤ To show/hide the grid, use **View - Grid** or `Ctrl` `Alt` `⇧ Shift` **G**.

▤ To show/hide the horizontal and vertical rulers, use **View - Rulers** or `Ctrl` `Alt` `⇧ Shift` **R**.

E-Undoing/redoing the last action

▤ To undo your last action, use **Edit - Undo** or ⬛ or `Ctrl` **Z**.

▤ To redo your last action, use **Edit - Redo** or `Ctrl` **Y** or ⬛.

F-Showing/hiding toolbars

▤ To show/hide a toolbar, use **Window - Toolbar**.

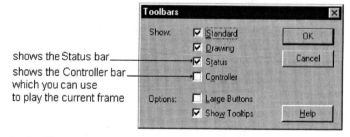

▤ In the **Show** list, activate/deactivate each option to show/hide the corresponding toolbar.

G-Using the inspectors

An inspector is a Flash tool that allows you to look at, organise and change the elements of a movie.

▤ Flash has four inspectors: **Object, Frame, Transform, Scene**. They are shown in an independent window, and thus enable you to see the contents of the movie at all times, making it easier to manage.

Window - Inspectors

Click the name of the inspector you want to display.

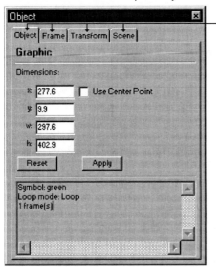

by default, all four inspectors are grouped in the same window

To show an inspector in a separate window, drag the inspector's tab out of the main window.

To group the inspectors in the same window, drag their tabs into the same window.

2.1 Graphic tools

A-Description of the Drawing toolbar

▓ The **Drawing** toolbar, situated on the left of the screen, allows you to draw, select, paint and edit graphic objects.

▓ The **Drawing** toolbar contains two parts:

(a)   The first part contains tools for drawing and selecting objects.

(b)   The second part allows you to refine the settings of the tool selected in the first part. Its contents change according to the selected tool.

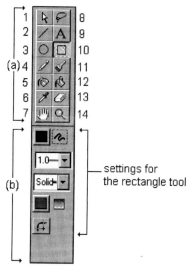

Number	Tool name	Shortcut key
1	Arrow	A
2	Line	
3	Oval	O
4	Pencil	P
5	Ink Bottle	I
6	Dropper	D
7	Hand	
8	Lasso	L
9	Text	T
10	Rectangle	R
11	Brush	B
12	Paint Bucket	U

Number	Tool name	Shortcut key
13	Eraser	E
14	Magnifier	M

▨ To activate a tool, click its button, or type the corresponding shortcut key. For most tools, a group of settings options appear in the bottom of the toolbar.

⇨ *If you want to activate a tool momentarily, use the shortcut keys given below. Once you release the key, the previous tool becomes active again.*

To momentarily activate:	Press:
Arrow (1)	Ctrl
Lasso (8)	⇄
Hand (7)	space
Zoom in	Ctrl
Zoom out	Ctrl ⇧ Shift space

B-Drawing and painting objects

Drawing a rectangle or square

▨ Click the **Rectangle** tool ▢ on the **Drawing** toolbar.

▨ If necessary, change the settings for this tool:

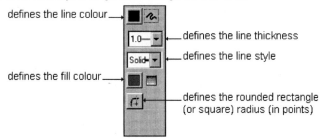

defines the line colour
defines the line thickness
defines the line style
defines the fill colour
defines the rounded rectangle (or square) radius (in points)

▨ Once you have chosen the settings, place the mouse pointer in the stage, click anywhere you like, and drag the pointer to another point in the stage, holding down the mouse button as you drag. Once you have drawn the rectangle you want, release the mouse button.

▨ If you want to draw a square (and not a rectangle), hold the ⇧ Shift key down as you draw.

A rectangle (or square) drawn in this way is composed of five objects. In fact, Flash breaks this geometric object down into four lines (four objects) that surround a fill (a fifth object). If you want to select the rectangle (or square) to edit or move it, you must select the five objects that compose it.

⇨ *Line thickness is measured in points. A point measures approximately 0.35 mm and 1 mm corresponds to roughly 2.83 points.*

Drawing a circle or an oval

▓ Click the **Oval tool** 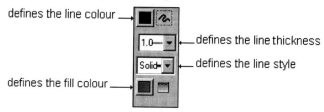 on the **Drawing** toolbar.

▓ If necessary, change the settings for this tool:

defines the line colour ⟶ — defines the line thickness

1.0

Solid — defines the line style

defines the fill colour ⟶

▓ Draw the oval by dragging.

▓ To draw a circle (and not an oval), hold the ⇧ Shift key down as you drag.

A circle (or oval) drawn in this way is made of two objects. Flash breaks this geometric shape down into a line (an object) and a fill (another object). If you want to select the circle (or oval) to edit or move it, you must select both the objects that compose it.

Drawing a straight line

▓ Click the **Line tool** on the **Drawing** toolbar.

▓ If necessary, change the settings for this tool:

colour ⟶

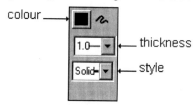

1.0 ⟵ thickness

Solid ⟵ style

▓ Draw the line by dragging.

▓ If you hold the ⇧ Shift key down as you drag, the line will be inclined at an angle of 45° to the vertical, horizontal or diagonal.

⇨ *When several straight lines join together to form an object (e.g. a triangle), you can colour the object in the same way as you would a rectangle or oval.*

⇨ *Be careful, the **Line*** 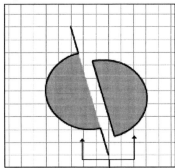 *tool acts like a knife when it crosses another object:*

└ the circle that has been crossed
.by a line splits into two distinct parts

Drawing with the Pencil tool

The **Pencil** tool in Flash 4 allows you to draw lines and shapes.

▦ Click the **Pencil** tool ✐ on the **Drawing** toolbar.

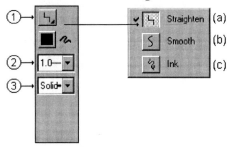

① Click the **Pencil Mode** button and choose one of the options:

(a)   to draw straight lines and/or convert approximate triangles, ovals, circles, rectangles and squares into exact geometric shapes.

(b)   to draw smooth curvy lines.

(c)   to draw freehand lines.

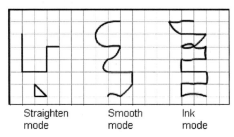

| Straighten mode | Smooth mode | Ink mode |

② Choose the thickness of the line.

③ Choose the line style.

▦ Draw the line by dragging.

⇨ *Hold the* Shift *key down as you drag to draw vertical or horizontal lines.*

⇨ *Lines created using the Pencil require less memory than those created using the Brush.*

2.2 Selections

A-Overview of selections

Depending on the selected element, the graphic representation of its selection changes. Selected fills and lines are cross-hatched, whereas selected groups and symbols are surrounded by a bounding box.

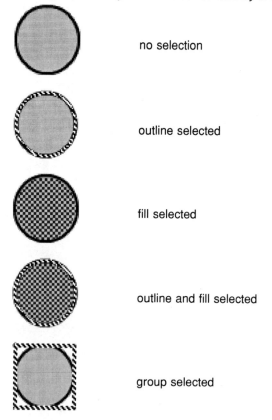

no selection

outline selected

fill selected

outline and fill selected

group selected

- To add to a current selection, hold the [⇧ Shift] key down before making additional selections. For this technique to work, the **Shift Select** option in **File - Preferences** must be active.
- If you want to select all the objects in each layer of the stage, use **Edit - Select All** or [Ctrl] **A**.
- To deselect everything, use **Edit - Deselect All** or [Ctrl][⇧ Shift] **A**.
- In order to protect a group or a symbol from accidental changes, you can lock it so that it cannot be selected. To do this, select the group or symbol in question, and use **Modify - Arrange - Lock** or [Ctrl][Alt] **L**.
- To unlock all the locked groups and symbols, use **Modify - Arrange - Unlock All** or [Ctrl][Alt][⇧ Shift] **L**.

B-Selecting using the Arrow tool

- Click the [⬆] tool on the **Drawing** toolbar to activate it, or press **A**.
- To select the fill and outline of a shape (such as a square), double-click the fill.
- To select a group of objects, drag to draw a frame around all the elements concerned. When you release the mouse, the selected objects are cross-hatched.

C-Selecting using the Lasso tool

Changing the Lasso settings

The Lasso tool [⌒] can be used individually to draw a freehand selection area, or can be combined with the Polygon modifier tool [⌒] to make a selection in polygon mode. Both these selection modes can be changed using the Magic wand [⬚].

- To make a precise selection, activate the **Lasso tool** [⌒], click the **Magic wand properties** tool [⬚], and in the associated list, choose the amount of **Smoothing** of the object borders: **Pixels, Rough, Normal** or **Smooth**.

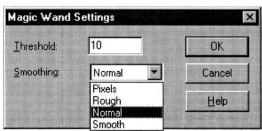

▓ So that Flash takes this rule into account as you are making a **Lasso** selection, activate the **Magic wand** tool ![magic wand icon].

Making a freehand selection

▓ Click the **Lasso tool** ![lasso icon] then, by dragging, draw a selection box around the part of the object you want to select. If you release the mouse before you have drawn around the whole selection, Flash 4 closes the gap with a straight line.

Making a selection in polygon mode

▓ Click the **Lasso tool** ![lasso icon] then click the **Polygon modifier** tool ![polygon icon].
▓ Click in the stage where the selection is to begin.
▓ Click where the first line should end.
▓ Now click the other stopping points to define the rest of the lines.
▓ Close the area selected in polygon mode by double-clicking.

Making a freehand selection in polygon mode

▓ Click the **Lasso tool** ![lasso icon], and deactivate the **Polygon modifier** tool ![polygon icon].
▓ To draw a straight line, hold down the ![Alt] key, click at the starting point then click the end point of the section.
▓ You can continue the selection by dragging freehand.
▓ To close the selection box, release the mouse button if you are completing a freehand section, or double-click for a straight section.

freehand selection

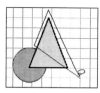

polygon mode selection

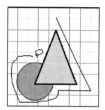

freehand selection in polygon mode

2.3 Managing objects

A- Grouping/ungrouping objects

▓ If you want to group objects, select them, and use **Modify - Group** or `Ctrl` **G**.

Ojects grouped in this way can be moved together.

▓ To ungroup objects, select them, and use **Modify - Ungroup** or `Ctrl` `⇧ Shift` **G**.

The ungrouped objects become independent and can be manipulated individually.

ungrouped, selected objects

grouped, selected objects

⇨ *If you want to keep an object outside of a group, convert it into a symbol by pressing* `F8`, *or place it in a different layer.*

⇨ *To optimise a movie's size, group the component objects as much as possible.*

B-Modifying an object

▓ To modify an object that is composed of a fill and an outline, activate the **Arrow** tool and place the mouse pointer near the outline of the object you want to modify.

Notice that the reshaping cursor appears:

 if the pointer is close to a corner,

if the pointer is anywhere else.

▓ If necessary, activate one of the options associated with the **Arrow** tool on the **Drawing** toolbar.

▓ Drag the object's border according to how you want to change it, and release the mouse when you achieve the appearance you want.

original object

as you change

after the change

⇨ *Remember that the **Undo** command in the **Edit** menu, or* Ctrl *Z, can be used to undo your last action.*

C-Changing an object's border

▨ Select the section you want to change using the **Arrow** tool.

▨ Click the ⬚ tool to **Smooth** the section, or the ⬚ tool to **Straighten** a curve.

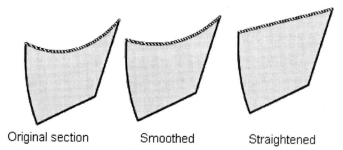

Original section   Smoothed   Straightened

D-Aligning/distributing/resizing objects

*The **Align** command in the **Modify** menu allows you to align several objects on the stage, and also to resize them so that they are of identical size. Another feature of this command is the option to space the selected objects evenly, if you want to.*

▨ Select the objects you want to align.

▨ **Modify - Align** or ⬚ or Ctrl K

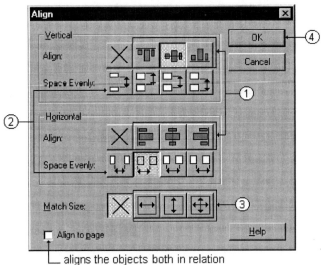

aligns the objects both in relation
to each other and in relation to the stage

① Choose the type of vertical or horizontal alignment.

② If you want to distribute the objects so that their centres, left or top borders, or right and bottom borders are evenly spaced, activate one of these options.

③ To resize the selected objects so that their horizontal and/or vertical dimensions are identical, activate one of these options. In this case, the selected objects are adjusted to the size of the largest object.

④ Confirm your changes.

⇨ *The alignment options can be used individually or in combination with others.*

E-Using the Snap tool for aligning objects

The Snap tool 🔲 *is situated on the Standard toolbar, or as a supplementary option for some buttons on the Drawing toolbar. This tool enables you to draw objects that will be automatically aligned with each other and on the grid on the stage. When the Snap tool is active, a small black circle accompanies the mouse pointer while you are dragging an object. The circle becomes thicker if two points can be aligned and adjusted precisely on the grid.*

indicates as you are moving
that the squares can be
precisely aligned on the grid

As you move or change the shape of objects, the position of the Arrow
tool on the object gives the reference point for the black ring.

▓ To activate/deactivate the **Snap** modifier, click the [▦] tool, or use
View - Snap or [Ctrl][Alt] **G**.

▓ To change the sensitivity of the **Snap** tool, use **File - Assistant** and
choose one of the options in the **Snap to grid** list.

⇨ *To be sure that Flash 4 snaps to the grid as you drag, start dragging*
from a corner or from the central point of the object in question.

F-Rotating/resizing an object

Rotating an object

▓ Select the object(s) you want to change using the **Arrow** ([▨]) or **Lasso**
([◉]) tool.

▓ To rotate the selected object (or group of objects), click the [↺] tool.
This tool activates round handles around the selection.

▓ Click one of the corner handles and, without releasing the mouse, drag
the selection to the angle you want then release the mouse.
If you hold the [⇧ Shift] key down as you drag, the rotation will be made in
45° steps.

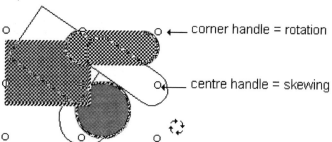

Resizing an object

▓ To resize the selected object (or group of objects), click the [▣] tool.
This tool activates rectangular handles around the selection.

▓ Click one of the corner handles and, without releasing the mouse, drag it
to reduce or increase the size of the selection then release the mouse
when you achieve the size you want.

The corner handles allow you to resize the selection proportionally, and
the centre handles stretch or squash the object in the direction they indi-
cate.

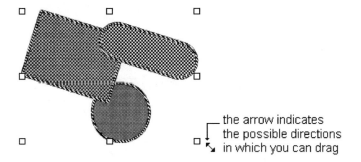

the arrow indicates
the possible directions
in which you can drag

G-Managing curves

Smoothing a curve

▓ Select the curve, and use **Modify - Curves** then choose the **Smooth** option.

Converting a curve to a fill

▓ Select the curve and use **Modify - Curves** and choose the **Lines to Fills** option.
The curve is converted into a filled shape.

▓ You can now resize the shape, if you like: deselect the curve then drag to change its thickness.

⇨ *Converting a curve to a fill may increase the size of files, but can also speed up the displaying of the drawing.*

Expanding the shape of a filled curve

▓ If you have not already done so, convert the curve to a fill.

▓ Select the filled curve, and use **Modify - Curves** and choose **Expand Shape**.

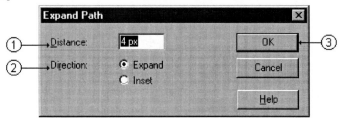

① Indicate by how much to expand the shape (in pixels).

② Choose **Expand** to increase the size of the shape or **Inset** to decrease its size.

③ Confirm your choice.

Softening the edges of a filled curve

▓ If you have not already done so, convert the curve to a fill.

▓ Select the curve, and use **Modify - Curves** then choose **Soften Edges**.

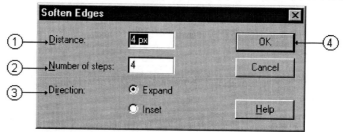

① Indicate by how much to soften the edges.

② Enter the number of curves to be used to soften the edges.

③ Choose **Expand** to increase the size of the shape, or **Inset** to decrease it.

④ Confirm your choices.

⇨ *The more steps you enter, the more the edges are softened, but this makes your files bigger and longer to draw.*

H-Using the Eraser

▓ To erase all the contents of a scene, double-click the **Eraser** tool .

▓ To erase a section of a line or fill, activate the **Eraser** and **Faucet** tools then click the line or fill you want to clear.

▓ To delete objects by dragging, activate the **Eraser** then the **Eraser Mode** tool .

▓ If necessary, deactivate the **Faucet** tool .

Click one of the options offered:

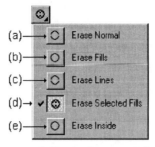

(a)   Erase Normal
(b)   Erase Fills
(c)   Erase Lines
(d)   Erase Selected Fills
(e)   Erase Inside

(a)   to erase lines and fills in the same layer by dragging in the usual way.

(b)   to erase only fills, leaving the lines untouched.

(c)   to erase only lines, leaving the fills untouched.

(d)   to erase only the selected fills, leaving the lines untouched, whether they are selected or not.

(e)   to erase only the fill where the eraser is, leaving the lines untouched.

▓ Click the arrow on the [■ ▼] tool to choose the shape and size of the eraser.

▓ In the scene, click the place concerned by the deletion, and, without releasing the mouse, drag around the area you want to clear. Release the mouse button to see the result.

⇨ *If you start erasing in an empty area, nothing will be cleared.*

I- Using the Hand and Zoom tools

▓ To zoom in or out on the stage, click the **Zoom** tool [🔍] then activate the **Enlarge** [⊕] or **Reduce** [⊖] tools, depending on what you want to do.

▓ Click on the stage where you want to zoom in or out.

▓ To define a precise zoom value, type a percentage in the **Zoom Control** [100% ▼] text box on the Standard toolbar.

▓ To move the stage so that you can see a hidden part of it, click the **Hand** tool [✋] then drag to move the stage.

▓ If you want to change to a tool other than [✋] momentarily, press [space].

▓ To zoom in on part of the stage, activate the **Magnifier** tool then draw a rectangle by dragging: Flash zooms in on the selected area so that it fills the window.

DRAWING AND GRAPHIC OBJECTS

2.4 Colours

A- Using the Brush tool

*The **Brush** tool enables you to apply colours to the stage using several brush shapes and drawing modes.*

▓ Click the **Brush** tool 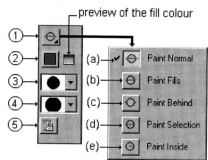 on the **Drawing** toolbar.

▓ Define the different options associated with the **Brush**:

① Click the **Brush Mode** tool then one of the modes suggested:

(a)   to paint normally over lines and fills in the same layer.

(b)   to paint filled areas and empty areas, without touching lines.

(c)   to paint the empty parts of the stage, without touching lines and fills.

(d)   to paint the selected fill.

(e)   to paint the fill without touching the lines.

② Define the brush's fill colour (solid or gradient).

③ Choose the size of the brush from the associated list.

④ Choose the shape of the brush from the associated list.

⑤ Click this tool if you want to activate the **Lock Fill** modifier (see 2.4 - F - Locking a gradient fill).

▓ Drag the brush on the stage.

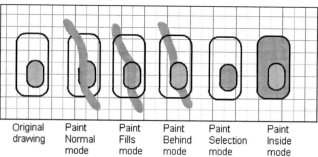

| Original drawing | Paint Normal mode | Paint Fills mode | Paint Behind mode | Paint Selection mode | Paint Inside mode |

⇨ *If you start to paint in an empty area, the brush will not paint in areas that are already filled.*

⇨ *Lines created using the Pencil require less memory than those created using the Brush.*

B-Using the Ink Bottle tool

The Ink Bottle tool enables you to change the outline of an object.

▓ Click the **Ink Bottle** tool.

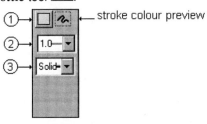

stroke colour preview

① To change the **Line Color**, click here then select a colour from the palette. By default, the last colour you used is selected.

② If necessary, click the arrow and choose the **Line Thickness**.

③ If necessary, click the arrow and choose the **Line Style**.

▓ Click the object whose borders you want to change according to the settings you have defined.

C-Using the colour palette

Depending on the active drawing or painting tool, Flash 4 offers one or two colour modifiers.

Active tool	Stroke (or Line) Color modifier ■ ✎	Fill Color modifier □ ▧
Pencil ✎	yes	
Line ╱	yes	
Rectangle □	yes	yes
Oval ○	yes	yes
Brush ✔		yes
Paint Bucket ◊		yes
Ink Bottle ◊	yes	

*So that you can differentiate between modifiers, notice that the **Line Co-**
lor modifier is followed by the [symbol], and the **Fill Color** modifier is
followed by [symbol].*

▓ To activate the colour palette, click the **Fill** (or **Line**) **Color** tool [symbol].

click here to draw filled or unfilled
shapes with no outline (none value)

click here to customise
solid or gradient colours

selected colour

current
palette

available gradient (accessible
via the Fill Color modifier)

preview of the colour

colour space

Color

Solid | Gradient

hue bar

R: 51
G: 51
B: 204

Snap to Web Safe

New   Delete   ☐ Hex   Change

Alpha 100 %

tick this option to translate the RGB codes
into hexadecimal values

deletes the selected colour table

allows you to choose the closest corresponding
colour in the standard 216 colour Web palette

⇨ *By default, the palette proposed by Flash 4 is the Web Safe (or Web 216) palette, which is made up of 216 colours that are supported by all browsers.*

Creating or editing a solid colour

▨ Display the colour palette by clicking the ⬚ tool then ⊞, or use **Window - Colors**.

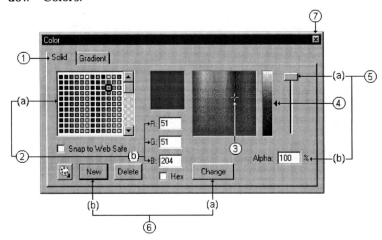

① Activate this tab.

② To select the colour you want to change, click in the table (a), or enter the value of its Red, Green and Blue components (b).

③ Drag the cross to move it and define the hue.

④ Drag the cursor to define the shade and brightness.

⑤ To define the transparency of the selected colour, slide the **Alpha** cursor (a) or type a percentage value (b). The value **0** corresponds to complete transparency.

⑥ To replace the selected colour by the colour you have just defined, click the **Change** button (a) and to save the new colour in the colour table, click **New** (b).

⑦ Close the dialog box and save the changes you have made.

Creating and editing a gradient

▨ Display the colour palette by clicking the ⬚ tool then ⊞, or use **Window - Colors**.

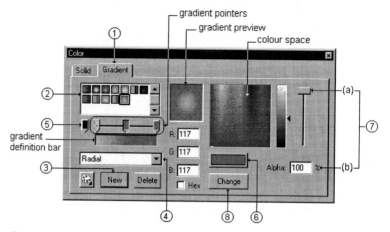

gradient pointers
gradient preview
colour space

① Activate this tab.

② Click a gradient to select it.

③ To change the selected gradient, go straight to point ④; If you want to create a new gradient based on the selected gradient, click here.

④ Open the list and chose **Radial** for a circular gradient or **Linear** for a gradient made up of lines.

⑤ To add a pointer to the gradient definition bar, drag a pointer from the **pointer well** onto the bar. The pointers indicate where the gradient changes colour.

⑥ Click to show the solid colours palette, and select the colour to be shown at the active colour pointer (the one which is pressed in). The pointer and the definition bar are instantly updated.

⑦ To define the transparency of the selected colour, drag the **Alpha** cursor (a) or type a percentage (b). The value **0** corresponds to complete transparency, and each colour that makes up the gradient can have its own level of Alpha setting.

⑧ Confirm your choices.

⇨ *To delete a colour pointer from the gradient definition bar, drag it off the bar.*

D-Importing/exporting colour palettes

Importing a colour palette

▓ Begin by opening the **Color** dialog box using the **Colors** command in the **Window** menu.

▓ Click the 🌐 button to open the pop-up menu, and choose the **Add Colors** option to integrate imported colours into the current palette, or **Replace Colors** to replace the current colours.

- Locate the colour file you want in the **Import Color Swatch** window then click **Open**.

Exporting a colour palette

- **Window - Colors**

- Click the 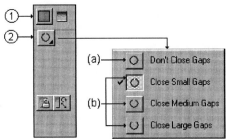 button to open the pop-up menu then choose **Save Colors**.
- In the **Export Color Swatch** window, type the **File name** of your colour palette, and choose an option from the **Save as type** list: **Flash Color Set (*clr)** or **Color Table (*.act)**.
- Click **Save**.

⇨ *CLR (Flash Color Set) files, which contain RGB colours and gradients, and ACT (Adobe Color Table) files, which contain only RGB colours, can be imported and exported. Files in ACT format can be used with Macromedia Fireworks and Adobe Photoshop. You can also import colour palettes (without gradients) from GIF files.*

⇨ *To restore the standard Web colour palette, activate **Web 216** in the menu on the button.*

E-Using the Paint Bucket tool

*The **Paint Bucket** tool allows you to fill a closed area (empty or already filled) with a solid colour, gradient, or bitmap. If you use a gradient or bitmap, the **Paint Bucket** tool enables you to adjust the direction of the centre of the fill.*

Filling an area

- Click the **Paint Bucket** tool.

① Display the colour palette and choose the fill colour (see 2.4 - C - Using the colour palette).

② Click the **Gap Size** button then activate one of the options:

(a)   if you want to close gaps yourself, which can save time in complex drawings.

(b)   so that Flash considers the gap closed. For this feature to work, the gaps should not be too wide.

▓ Click the shape or the closed area.

Adjusting a gradient or bitmap fill

▓ Click the **Paint Bucket** tool ![icon] then the **Transform Fill** tool ![icon].

The mouse pointer takes this shape: ⬚ .

▓ Click in an area filled with a gradient or bitmap.

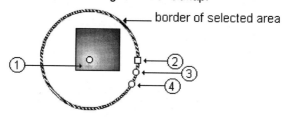

border of selected area

When you point to one of the proposed edit handles, the pointer shows you its function.

① To reposition the area's centre point, click then, without releasing the mouse, drag the centre point to its new position: the pointer takes this shape: ✛ .

② Drag this edit handle to change the width (or height) of the fill. The pointer takes this shape: ↔ .

③ Drag this edit handle to change the radius of a circular gradient. The pointer takes this shape: ↺ .

④ Drag this edit handle to rotate the fill. The pointer takes this shape: ↻ .

⇨ *To see all the handles when you are working with large filled areas, or when they are close to the edge of the stage, use* **View - Work Area.**

F- Locking a gradient fill

The principle and use of a locked gradient

The principle of using a locked gradient is to use a predefined gradient as a colour and position reference on the stage.

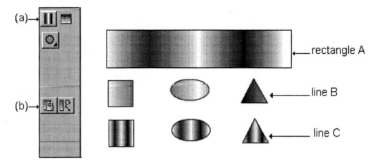

In this example, first a reference area was created (rectangle A), using the gradient (a) which was locked (b).

To fill the objects on line B, the **Paint Bucket** tool was used with the <u>fill locked</u>. Notice the resizing effect on the gradient, giving the impression that the objects are extracts of rectangle A.

For the objects on line C, the **Paint Bucket** tool was used without activating the fill lock. The objects' fill has not been resized.

Using a locked gradient

▓ Click the **Brush tool** 🖌 or the **Paint Bucket** tool 🪣 then choose (or create) a gradient (see 2.4 - C - Using the colour palette).

▓ Click the **Lock Fill** tool 🖵.

▓ First, paint the area(s) that will be the centre of the filled area (reference area).

▓ Now paint the other areas.

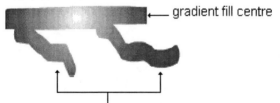

gradient fill centre

objects added with the locked gradient

G-Using the Dropper tool

The **Dropper** tool is used to copy a fill and lines of an object to another object.

▓ Click the **Dropper** tool 🖉 then the object whose fill and line attributes you want to copy.

If you have clicked a line, the **Ink Bottle** tool is activated. The **Paint Bucket** and **Lock Fill** tools are activated if you have clicked a fill.

▧ Click the object to which you want to apply the previously copied formatting.

⇨ *If you hold the* 【⇧ Shift】 *key down when you click with the **Dropper** tool, the formatting of the copied fill and lines is applied to the modifiers of all the drawing tools.*

2.5 Text

If the character font used in your movie is not available on the viewer's computer, display problems might arise. To overcome this, Flash 4 replaces _sans, _serif and _typewriter fonts with the browser's standard fonts. You can also convert selected text into vector graphics before you export your movie.

A-Entering text

▧ Click the **Text** tool ◪.

▧ Choose the formatting attributes of your characters (see 2.5 - C - Formatting characters).

▧ To create a one-line text block that increases as you type, click in the work area and start to type.

> Eni Publishing offers you computing books for all levels⌐

The text block increases in size as you type your text.

▧ To create a text block with a fixed width, draw the block by dragging then type your text inside.

> Eni Publishing offers you computing books for all levels

As the width of the text block is fixed, line breaks are automatic.

▧ As you enter text, use the arrow keys or the mouse to move the cursor around the text, and make any necessary corrections.

▧ To change the size of a text block, drag the handle on the <u>top right</u> corner. This handle is round if the block does not have a fixed width, and square if it does.

⇨ *When text is entered, corrected, and formatted, you can convert it into a vector graphic in order to apply any graphic features you want. Text can also be converted into vectors if it is to be animated in a movie.*

B-Creating a Text field

A text field enables you to put editable text into a movie, meaning that users can edit the text while they are watching your movie. When you create a text field, it is assigned a variable. This variable can be exploited using JavaScript, or another language used on the Internet.

▓ Click the **Text tool**  then the **Text Field** tool [abi].

▓ Drag to draw the text field.

Notice that the drag handle is found in the bottom right corner and that a black border surrounds the block.

▓ If necessary, use **Modify - Text Field** or [Ctrl][Alt] **F**, to change the text field's properties.

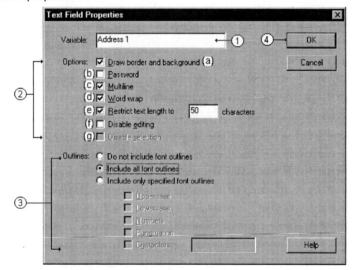

① Type the name of the text field.

② If necessary, activate the following options:

(a)	to draw a border and background for the text field.
(b)	if you want the text entered in the field by a user to be replaced by asterisks.
(c)	to enable line breaks when a user enters text.
(d)	to insert line breaks automatically when the text reaches the right hand margin of the published movie.
(e)	to limit the number of characters to the specified number.
(f)	to prevent other users from editing the field. Use this option if you want to display text dynamically.

(g)   to prevent users from selecting text in the field.

③ Choose whether to include all the font outlines, none of them or only those specified. If you want to optimise the size of your movie, it is best to include only the specified outlines rather than all of them.

④ Confirm your settings.

⇨ *To transform an ordinary text block into a text field, after activating the*

Text tool, click inside the block then click the Text Field tool ![abl]. *Immediately, the drag handle moves to the bottom right hand corner. Define the text field properties using the menu Modify - Text Field.*

C-Formatting characters

▓ Click the **Text** tool ![A].

▓ If the text you want to format has already been entered, select it by dragging. If not, the formatting you chose previously will be applied to the text you type.

▓ Choose the options you want:

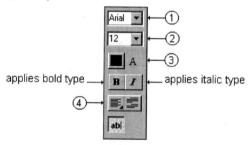

applies bold type ———→   ←——— applies italic type

① Open the character font list and click the font you want.

② Choose the size of the characters (defined in points).

③ If necessary, change the colour by selecting a shade from the colour palette.

④ Click this button to open the associated pop-up menu and choose the alignment of the text in relation to the borders: **Left**, **Center**, **Right** or **Justify**.

▓ Click the ![button] button to define the paragraph properties:

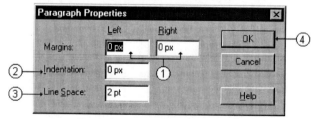

① Enter the space to leave between the edges of the text and the edges of the text box, in pixels.

② Enter the space to leave between the paragraph's left margin and the start of the first line, in pixels.

③ Enter the space to leave between consecutive lines of the paragraph, in points.

④ Confirm your choices.

⇨ *The formatting options are also available via the menus **Modify - Font** and **Modify - Paragraph**.*

⇨ *To check that the font you have chosen can be exported with a movie, use **View - Antialias Text** (or* Ctrl Alt ⇧ Shift *T). If the text remains jagged, Flash does not recognise the font and will not be able to export the text.*

⇨ *To optimise the size of a movie, try to limit the number of fonts and styles you use.*

D-Converting text into shapes

Flash 4 can ungroup text to convert it into shapes. Only entire text blocks can be converted into shapes.

▓ Click the **Arrow** tool [ ] then the text block concerned.

▓ **Modify - Break Apart**

The characters are converted into lines and fills, and can no longer be edited as text.

Characters converted in this way can be changed in the same way as any other shape.

⇨ *This feature can only be used with outline fonts such as TrueType fonts. Bitmap fonts disappear from the screen when you ungroup them. PostScript fonts can only be ungrouped with Adobe Type Manager on a Macintosh.*

2.6 Importing

A-Overview

In Flash, you can import graphic objects in a large variety of vector and bitmap format files.

Before importing a bitmap graphic, you should check its size and resolution. The dimensions of the images should not exceed the size of the display area, and a resolution of 72 ppi is quite sufficient for the Internet.

If you want to import an image sequence (PICT or BMP format), be sure that the sequence of the pictures is easily identifiable. To do this, number the images, because when you import them you will be importing them as a succession of images.

Importing bitmap and vector graphics can be done using the clipboard, but it is preferable to export the data from the source program into a file which will then be imported into Flash. By doing this, you can edit the file using other applications before importing it into your Flash movie.

DIFFERENT GRAPHIC FORMATS		
Image types	File types	Import into Flash 4 under Windows
Adobe Illustrator	.eps, .ai	yes
Animated GIF	.gif	yes
GIF	.gif	yes
AutoCAD DXF	.dxf	yes
Bitmap	.bmp	yes
Enhanced Metafile	.emf	yes
FutureSplash	.spl	yes
JPEG	.jpg	yes
PICT	.pct, .pic	no
PNG	.png	yes
Flash	.swf	yes
Windows Metafile	.wmf	yes
QuickTime Movie	.mov	yes

B-Importing a file

Importing a file

▓ **File - Import** or ⌨ **R**

▓ In the **Import** dialog box, select the file you want to import and click **Open**.

The contents of the file appear on the stage. Depending on the type of file, you may be able to add it to the Library but this does not mean that

the file is a symbol. You can work directly with the image, resize it, rotate it, etc.

Importing a sequence

- **File - Import** or Ctrl R

- In the **Import** dialog box, select the file you want to import and click **Open**.

- If the file you are importing ends with a number and, in the same folder, Flash detects a sequence of images, a message will appear asking you if you want to import the whole sequence or just the selected image.

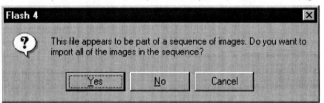

- Click **Yes** or **No**, depending on your intentions.

Importing an image using the clipboard

- To paste an image from another application, copy it in the source program, then use **Edit - Paste** in Flash 4.

- To paste an image as an embedded object, copy it in the source program, then use **Edit - Paste Special** in Flash 4.
  Any editing you do to such an object will be done in the source application, which you can activate by double-clicking the object (see Importing a graphic object using OLE, below).

⇨ *So that Flash can rotate an embedded bitmap, you must first select it, then use* ***Modify - Break Apart***.

⇨ *To import a FreeHand 8 graphic using the clipboard, select the CMYK and RGB options in the FreeHand export preferences.*

Importing a graphic object using OLE

In Windows, OLE (Object Linking and Embedding) is a technique that enables you to insert objects from one application into another application.

As long as your Flash movie has not been exported as a Shockwave file, your computer needs two applications to manage an imported object. However, once you have exported your movie, the link to the source program disappears, and the movie works normally.

- For example, to import Excel data using OLE, first save your movie.

- Click the **Arrow tool**.

- Right-click the stage to open the context menu.

- Click the **Insert Object** command in the context menu.

The *Insert Object* window opens, listing all the applications that manage OLE features.

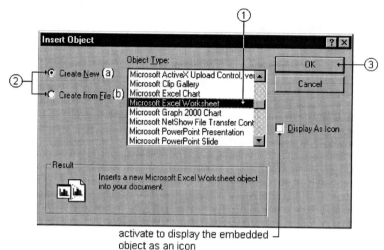

activate to display the embedded
object as an icon

① Select the application you want to use. In this example, Microsoft Excel has been chosen.

② Choose whether to insert a new object (a), or to insert an existing file (b). In the second instance, give the file name.

③ Confirm the insertion of the object. The menus and toolbars of Flash are replaced with those of the chosen application.

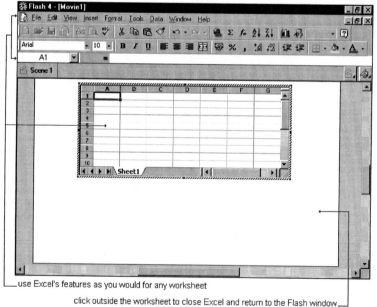

use Excel's features as you would for any worksheet

click outside the worksheet to close Excel and return to the Flash window

After you have created the new object using the features of another application (Microsoft Excel in this case), and closed the OLE window, the object is saved in the current Flash project, but is unavailable in Microsoft Excel.

▓ To animate an OLE object, save it as a Symbol in the Library, then work with it as you would a symbol created in Flash.

▓ If you need to make changes to the data, select the object concerned and use **Edit - Edit Selected** to reopen the link to the source application. You can also double-click the object in question.

3.1 The Timeline

A-Discovering the Timeline window

The Flash Timeline window is an essential tool for defining the settings for creating movies.

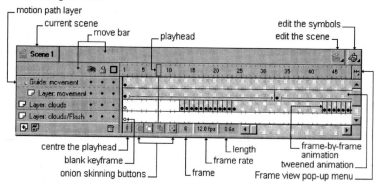

The Timeline window is made up of two parts. In the right part are the layer-by-layer and frame-by-frame operations. These appear in chronological order. In the left part, the layers determine the order of the objects.

Moving the playhead

▦ Drag the playhead to the required position, or simply click the number of the frame concerned.

Moving the Timeline window

▦ Drag the move bar to where you want to place the Timeline window.

If you move the Timeline window near the edges of your screen, it will dock in the Flash window, otherwise it will remain floating.

⇨ *To that the Timeline window does not dock in the Flash window, hold the* Ctrl *key down as you drag.*

Changing the Timeline display

▓ Click the [▥] tool at the right of the Timeline header to display the **Frame View** pop-up menu and choose the option you want:

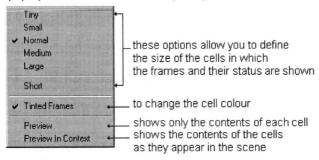

Tiny
Small
✔ Normal
Medium
Large

Short

✔ Tinted Frames

Preview
Preview In Context

these options allow you to define the size of the cells in which the frames and their status are shown

to change the cell colour

shows only the contents of each cell
shows the contents of the cells as they appear in the scene

▓ The **Preview** option does not show all the keyframes: if you insert a white graphic onto a black stage, it will not be visible because the colour of the stage is not an element in the cells.

⇨ *To increase the height of a layer, double-click the symbol that precedes its name in the Timeline window and change the* **Layer Height** *value in the* **Layer Properties** *dialog box.*

B-Discovering layers

▓ In the Timeline window, layers are shown in the left of the window and are stored in a hierarchical order.

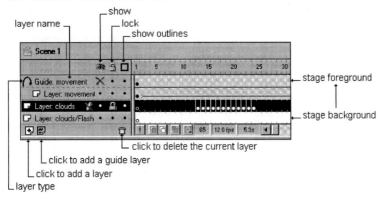

show
layer name
lock
show outlines

Scene 1

Guide: movement
Layer: movement
Layer: clouds
Layer: clouds/Flash
stage foreground
stage background
65 12.0 fps 5.3s

click to delete the current layer
click to add a guide layer
click to add a layer
layer type

▓ Imagine that each layer is a transparent sheet, and that they are stacked on top of each other on the stage.

▓ Objects placed in a layer will cover any objects in lower layers.

▓ Flash generates an empty layer when you open a new movie, and you can add as many layers as you want. The number of layers does not affect the size of your files, but their contents do.

MOVIE PRINCIPLES

- When you create a graphic on the stage, the current cell in the selected layer receives the graphics, which means you are drawing in the layer. You can draw and edit objects in a layer without making any changes to the other layers.
- You are strongly recommended to use separate layers for actions and sound files. This means that you will be able to access the actions or sounds more rapidly if you need to make any changes.
- It is also useful to know that you can lock or hide layers to make it easier to create effects.
- There are different types of layer:

Normal this is an ordinary layer in which you can insert graphics, sounds and animations. By default, all new layers are **Normal**.

Guide this is a layer in which you can insert help tools or objects that will help you to place others (such as a motion path). A guide layer is linked to other layers that contain objects that are arranged according to those in the guide. A guide layer is indicated by a symbol in front of the name of the layer: if the guide has not yet been linked to another layer, the ⌐ symbol is shown, and the ⌂ symbol denotes a guide that is associated with another layer.

Guided a guided layer is linked to a guide layer.

Mask a Mask layer hides everything in the other layers that are linked to it, except where you place a filled object. The filled shape or text object in the Mask layer creates a hole through which you can see the contents of the layers beneath. A Mask layer contains only a shape, instance or type object.

Masked this type of layer is linked to a mask layer. Its contents behave normally.

⇨ *To optimise the size of your movie, you are advised to use layers to differentiate between elements that change during the movie and those that do not.*

C-Managing layers

Creating a new layer

- Click the ⊞ button in the bottom left of the Timeline window, or use **Insert - Layer**.

The new layer is inserted above the active layer.

Selecting layers

- To select a layer, you can click its name in the Timeline window, click a frame in the Timeline, or select an object on the stage.

▓ To select several layers, hold the ⟦⇧ Shift⟧ key down, and click the first then last layer you want to select in the Timeline window. To select non-adjacent layers, hold the ⟦Ctrl⟧ key down and click the layers you want to select.

Deleting a layer

▓ Select the layer concerned.

▓ Drag it to the 🗑 button, or simply click the 🗑 button.

Deleting a layer also deletes its contents. If the layer contains instances, they are deleted with the layer, but the corresponding symbols will still be available in the Library.

Copying a layer

▓ Click the name of the layer you want to copy to select all of it and not just one of its components.

▓ **Edit - Copy Frames** or ⟦Ctrl⟧⟦Alt⟧ **C**

▓ Click the ⊞ button to create a new layer.

▓ Click in the new layer and use **Edit - Paste Frames** or ⟦Ctrl⟧⟦Alt⟧ **V**.

Changing the order of layers

▓ To move a layer in the Timeline window, drag it to its new position.

As you drag, a horizontal cross-hatched bar indicates the new position of the layer.

Locking/unlocking a layer

A locked layer cannot be edited.

▓ To lock a layer, click to the right of its name in the column that carries the padlock symbol.

▓ Unlock the layer by clicking in the same place.

▓ To lock all the layers, click the 🔒 icon, and click it again to unlock the layers.

➪ *If you hold the ⟦Alt⟧ key down as you click in the Lock column of a layer, all the other layers will be locked, but not the one you clicked. Clicking again will unlock the layers.*

Renaming a layer

▓ Double-click the name of the layer you want to rename.

▓ Type the new name then press ⟦Enter⟧ .

Managing a layer's properties

▓ Double-click the icon to the left of the layer's name.

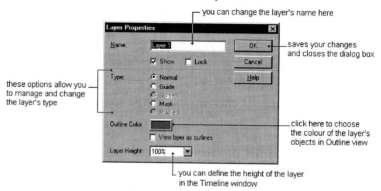

these options allow you to manage and change the layer's type

you can change the layer's name here

saves your changes and closes the dialog box

click here to choose the colour of the layer's objects in Outline view

you can define the height of the layer in the Timeline window

D-Discovering the cells in the Timeline

The cells in the Timeline window present what is happening in the different areas. In every new layer, Flash automatically inserts an empty keyframe into the first cell on the timeline header.

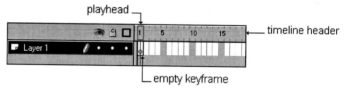

playhead

timeline header

empty keyframe

When you create an object on the stage, Flash automatically inserts a keyframe in the active layer (see 3.1 - A - Discovering the Timeline window).

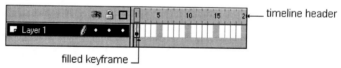

timeline header

filled keyframe

▓ To insert a keyframe into the active layer, press F6. Flash reproduces the active keyframe in a new cell. If you want to insert the keyframe in a particular place, click in the cell concerned before pressing F6.

Notice that the following cells are not shifted.

▓ To insert an empty frame into an existing sequence, press F5 rather than F6.

Flash shifts any animations to the right of the current position.

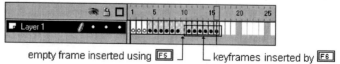

empty frame inserted using F5

keyframes inserted by F6

- To insert a series of keyframes, select the frames concerned by dragging before pressing F6.
- To insert several empty frames at once, press F5 after selecting as many cells as you want to insert.
- To delete a keyframe, click in the frame in question, and press ⇧ Shift F6.

  The frames that follow the active frame are not shifted because the keyframe is replaced by an empty cell.

  If you delete a keyframe that contains an object, the object is also deleted if it has not been saved as a symbol in the Library.

- To delete an empty frame, click the frame in question then press ⇧ Shift F5.

E-Representing movies in the Timeline

If a movie contains images that are not animated automatically, it is called a **frame-by-frame animation** (or **static animation**). Each frame contains an image, and when the frames are shown rapidly in sequence, they create an illusion of animation.

Animations that involve moving images from one point to another, with the intermediate steps interpreted by Flash, are called **motion tweening**.

An animation that follows the principle above, but can also involve changes in the colours, size and rotation of the start images, is called **shape tweening**.

The representation in the Timeline of these three main types of animation differs.

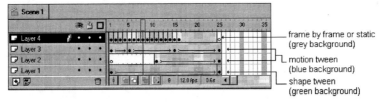

frame by frame or static (grey background)

motion tween (blue background)

shape tween (green background)

3.2 Symbols and instances

A-Discovering symbols and instances

- A **symbol** is an animation, graphic or button saved in a Library, meaning it can be used as many times as necessary. When you use a symbol in a movie, you are not actually using the symbol itself, but rather an **instance**. Flash does not reproduce the symbol completely, but refers to it.

- Using symbols in a movie considerably reduces the size of the file because saving several references to a symbol uses less disk space than a complete description of the symbol, repeated several times. It is recommended that you use symbols, animated or not, for any element that appears more than once so that you can optimise the size of your movie.

- When you change a symbol, the changes you make are automatically applied to all the instances of the symbol, which can be useful and save you time when a symbol is used several times in a movie. Inversely, changes made to an instance have no effect on the symbol.

- Using symbols often means that it will take a browser less time to read your movie, as the symbol will only be downloaded once, even if it occurs dozens of times.

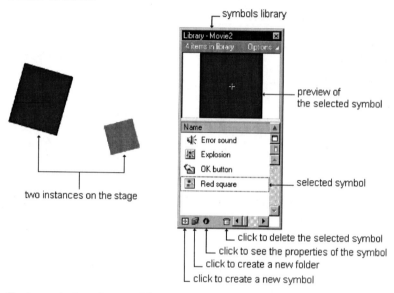

symbols library

preview of the selected symbol

selected symbol

two instances on the stage

click to delete the selected symbol
click to see the properties of the symbol
click to create a new folder
click to create a new symbol

Each movie has its own Library of symbols, and Flash 4 also offers you ready-made Libraries that are common to all movies. You can access them via the Libraries menu.

B-Creating a symbol

- Make sure that nothing on the stage is selected.
- **Insert - New Symbol** or [Ctrl] [F 8]

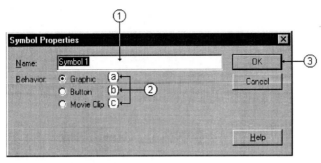

① Type the name of the symbol.

② Choose its **Behavior**:

(a) use this option for static images and when you want to create reusable items in a movie that are linked to the scenario of the main movie.

(b) this option is for interactive buttons that react to standard mouse actions, such as a click.

(c) use this option to create reusable items that run independently from the scenario of the main movie. This mini-movie can contain interactive controls, sounds, and, if you like, more instances of movie clips.

③ Confirm the creation of the symbol.

Flash activates symbol-editing mode.

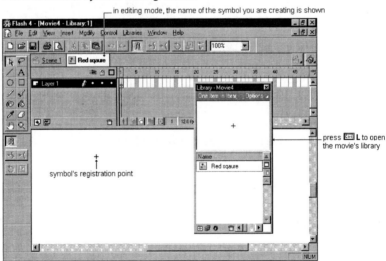

If you cannot see the symbol's registration point, use **View - Show Frame**.

▓ Create the contents of the symbol using the drawing tools or by importing an object, or even by creating instances of other symbols.

- Once you have created a symbol you are happy with, use **Edit - Edit Movie** or Ctrl **E** to leave symbol-editing mode.

⇨ *You can create a symbol from an existing element (or elements): select the elements in question and use **Insert - Convert to Symbol** or* Ctrl F8 *. Choose the type of symbol you want to create in the **Symbol Properties** dialog box and confirm with **OK**. The selected elements form one symbol.*

C-Managing symbols

- Open the movie's Library using **Window - Library** or Ctrl **L**.
- Click the name of the symbol in the Library to select it.
- Open the **Options** menu in the **Library** window.

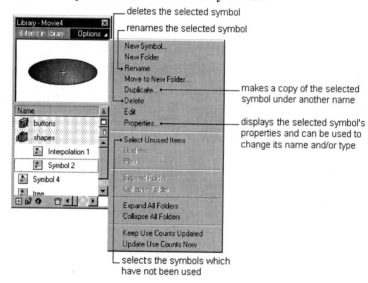

deletes the selected symbol

renames the selected symbol

makes a copy of the selected symbol under another name

displays the selected symbol's properties and can be used to change its name and/or type

selects the symbols which have not been used

⇨ *To make it easier to find your symbols you can create folders in the Library to store them. To do this, click the* ⬚ *button at the bottom of the **Library** window, and type the name of the folder. To file a symbol in a folder, drag it to the name of the folder you want.*

D-Using symbols from another movie

Each movie has its own Library of symbols. You can use a symbol from another Library in the current movie.

- Leave the current movie open.
- Open another movie's library using **File - Open as Library** or Ctrl ⇧ Shift **O**.
- Select the movie whose library you want to use and click **Open**.

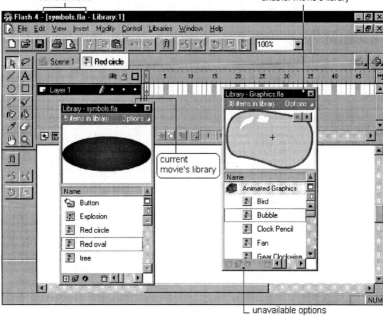

In the other movie's library, select the symbol you want to use and drag it into the current scene.

Flash 4 creates an instance of the symbol on the stage and copies the symbol into the current movie's library.

⇨ *Flash 4 is supplied with several preset libraries, which can usually be found in **Program Files\Macromedia\Flash 4\Libraries**. To open these libraries, use the **Libraries** menu.*

E- Creating and managing an instance of a symbol

Creating an instance

If you want to use a symbol from a Library in a scene, select the symbol in the Library and drag it onto the stage.

*Flash 4 creates an **instance** of the symbol.*

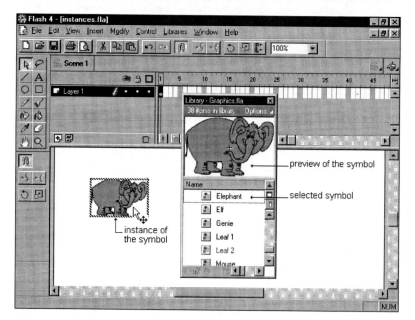

preview of the symbol

selected symbol

instance of the symbol

Changing a symbol and all its instances

▨ Using the ⎢⌖⎥ tool, select one of the instances concerned.

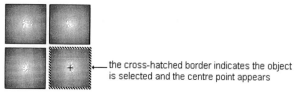

the cross-hatched border indicates the object is selected and the centre point appears

▨ Right-click the selection to open its context menu, or open the **Modify** menu.

here is an example of an un-separated instance's context menu

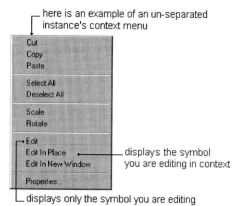

displays the symbol you are editing in context

displays only the symbol you are editing

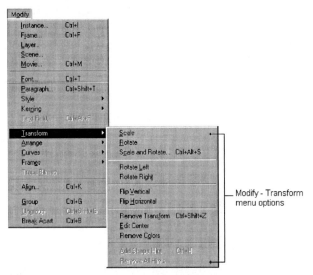

Modify - Transform
menu options

*The options **Rotate Left** and **Rotate Right** turn the object 90° to the left or right of its current angle. The rotation is in relation to its axis, indicated by a small cross. The **Edit Center** option allows you to move the object's central rotation axis.*

▓ To change the appearance of the symbol, use the standard formatting options to make your changes (see 2.3 - Managing objects).

▓ When you have finished, leave symbol editing mode using **Edit - Edit Movie** or [Ctrl] **E**, or click on the name of the current scene at the top of the Timeline window.

Flash changes the symbol and all its instances.

F-Changing an instance's properties

Each instance has its own properties, which are different from those of the symbol. An instance keeps any properties you have changed, even if you edit the symbol or link the instance to another symbol.

*To optimise the size of your movie, use the **Color Effect** pop-up menu in the **Instance Properties** dialog box to create several coloured instances of the same symbol.*

Changing the colour and the transparency

▓ Select the instance concerned using the [▶] or [✎] tool.

▓ **Modify - Instance** or double-click the instance.

▓ Activate the **Color Effect** tab.

▓ From the list associated with **Color Effect**, choose:

Brightness   to set the brightness of the image using the associated percentage scale.

MOVIE PRINCIPLES

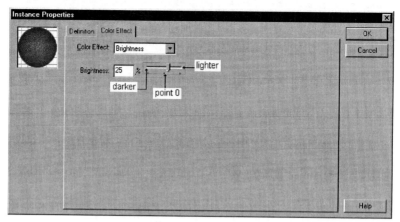

Tint to change the colour of the instance using this dialog box's options.

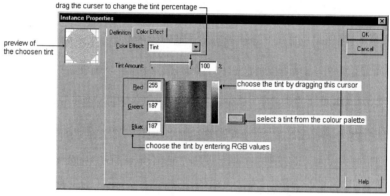

Alpha to change the transparency of the instance.

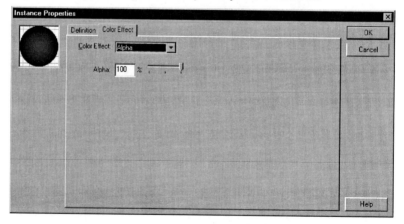

Special   to set the **Red, Green** and **Blue** values separately, and the instance's transparency.

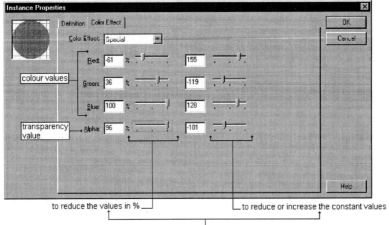

to reduce the values in % ⌐
to reduce or increase the constant values ⌐

to obtain new values, the current values are multiplied by the % values then added to the constant values

Changing an instance's type

▓ On the stage, select the instance concerned.

▓ **Modify - Instance** or Ctrl I

▓ Activate the **Definition** tab.

▓ Activate one of the options in the **Behavior** frame.

▓ Click **OK** to confirm and close the dialog box.

Associating an instance with a different symbol

▓ On the stage, select the instance whose symbol you want to change.

▓ **Modify - Instance** or Ctrl I

▓ Activate the **Definition** tab.

▓ In the list, select the replacement **Symbol**, then click the [⊙] button.

▓ Click **OK** to confirm and close the dialog box.

G-Separating an instance from its symbol

If you do want changes you make to one instance to be applied to all other instances and the symbol, you must separate the instance in question from its symbol before you edit it.

▓ Select the instance concerned using the [↖] or [✐] tool.

▓ **Modify - Break Apart** or Ctrl **B**

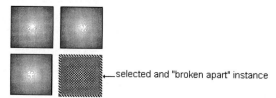
←selected and "broken apart" instance

■ Use the standard formatting tools (see 2.3 - Managing objects).

Notice that symbol editing mode is not active because you are editing an instance.

■ When you have finished making the changes, unselect the instance to see the result more clearly.

The changes you have made to the instance have no effect on the symbol or the other instances of the symbol. If you make any changes to the symbol in question, all its instances will be updated, except that which you have just edited.

4.1 Movies

A- Presentation of the different types of movie

There a three main types of movie in Flash 4.

▓ In a **frame-by-frame** (or **static**) animation, each frame contains a different image, and when the frame sequence is read rapidly, an animation effect is produced.

Principle:

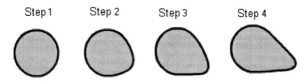

Step 1　　　Step 2　　　Step 3　　　Step 4

▓ Animations or image movements, which are automatically interpreted by Flash using a start point and an end point, use a technique called **motion tweening**.

Principle:

Start symbol　　　　　　　　End symbol and position

Flash interpolates the intermediate steps in a movement, which does not necessarily follow a straight line.

▓ When an animation that follows this last principle undergoes changes in colour, a rotation, or resizing, it is called **shape tweening**. This technique is comparable to morphing.

Principle:

Start image　　　　　　　　　　End image

Flash interpolates the intermediate steps

⇨ *Whenever possible, try to use interpolated movies, as they pose fewer problems than a series of keyframes.*

MAKING MOVIES

Some fundamental points

- A movie can contain several scenes, which are themselves composed of layers. For example, an action associated with a button might run another scene.
- Note that there is <u>only one animation per layer</u>.
- If you use sounds in your movies, be aware that Flash considers sounds to be animations, so must also apply the "one sound (animation) per layer" rule in this case.

B-Creating a movie and setting its properties

- File - **New** or ⌨ **N**

  *Flash creates a working file called **Movie**, followed by a number. This name is temporary, and you can rename the file when you save it.*

- **Modify** - **Movie** or ⌨ **M**

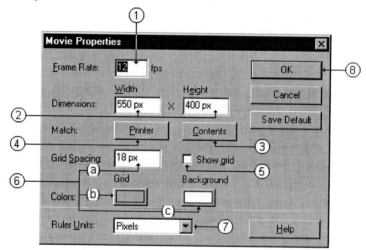

① Indicate the number of frames per second. If your movie is intended for use in a Web site, you should choose a rate between 8 and 12 fps (frames per second). On the other hand, if your movie is destined for a CD, you can choose a higher frame rate.

② Define the size of the dimensions of the stage in pixels, which must be at least 18 x 18 pixels and must not exceed 2880 x 2880 pixels. You are strongly recommended to choose dimensions adapted to your image, because the larger the surface of the image, the more disk space it uses.

③ Click this button to tell Flash to define equal spacing around the stage contents.

④ Click this button if you want to change the dimensions of the stage to fit the largest possible print area. This depends on the default settings and the **Size** of paper specified in the **File - Page Setup** dialog box, minus the current margins.

⑤ Activate this option to show the grid while you are editing, which will make it easier to place objects on the stage.

⑥ If necessary, change the value, in pixels, of the grid spacing (a), and click buttons (b) and (c) to choose the colours of the grid and background.

⑦ Click here to open the associated list then choose the unit of measurement for the ruler. By default, Flash uses pixels to indicate external dimensions, on the ruler and on the grid.

⑧ Confirm your choices.

⇨ *Remember that one inch equals 2.54 cm, and that 100 pixels is equal to 3.53 cm. Below you can see a list of the real dimensions of a browser window in relation to the chosen screen resolution:*

Screen resolution	Internal dimensions (in full screen mode)
640 x 480 pixels	600 x 300 pixels
800 x 600 pixels	760 x 420 pixels
1024 x 768 pixels	955 x 600 pixels

C-Saving a movie

Saving a new movie

▓ **File**
Save
or **Save As**

Ctrl S or
Ctrl ⇧ Shift S

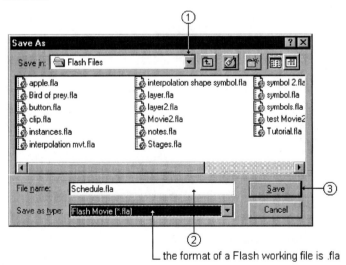

└ the format of a Flash working file is .fla

① Go to the drive where you want to save the movie, and open the folder concerned by double-clicking its name.

② Type the movie's name.

③ Save the movie.

Saving an existing movie

▓ File
   Save

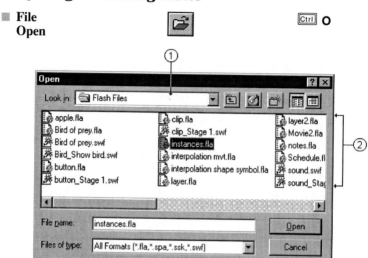

Ctrl S

D-Opening an existing movie

▓ File
   Open

Ctrl O

① Go to the drive where the movie is stored and open the folder by double-clicking its name.

② Double-click the name of the movie you want to open. A Flash working file carries the extension .fla and an exported movie has the extension .swf (see 6.2 - Exporting and publishing).

E-Creating a frame by frame animation

This type of movie is used when you need to change the image in each cell, which can be useful for complicated animations. Frame by frame movies require more disk space than interpolated movies.

▓ Click the name of the layer you want to activate in the Timeline window.

▓ Click the cell that corresponds to the starting point of the animation.

▓ Use **Insert - Keyframe** or ⌈F6⌋ if the cell does not already contain a keyframe.

The playhead is placed at the point you have selected and an empty keyframe icon appears.

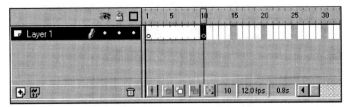

In this example, a keyframe has been inserted in the tenth frame of layer 1.

▨ Draw the first image of the sequence using Flash's drawing tools, or by importing an image (with or without the clipboard).

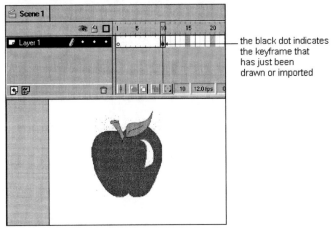

the black dot indicates the keyframe that has just been drawn or imported

▨ Click the cell to the right of the active frame then use **Insert - Keyframe** or F6 .

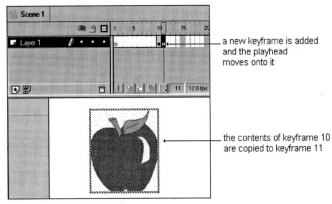

a new keyframe is added and the playhead moves onto it

the contents of keyframe 10 are copied to keyframe 11

▨ Change the contents of the image in the keyframe on the stage to create the next step in the animation.

▨ Continue your frame-by-frame movie by repeating the last two steps until the animation is finished.

MAKING MOVIES

Flash 4

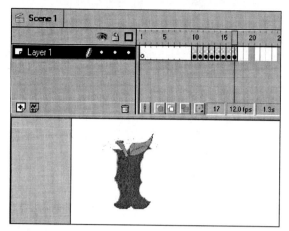

In this example, eight keyframes have been created to represent the eating of the apple.

▨ To test an animation, use **Control - Play** or Enter .

F-Testing a movie

Using the Onion Skin view

If you want to show several steps of an animation on the stage at once so that you can have more control over their changes and/or movements, use Flash's *Onion Skin tool*.

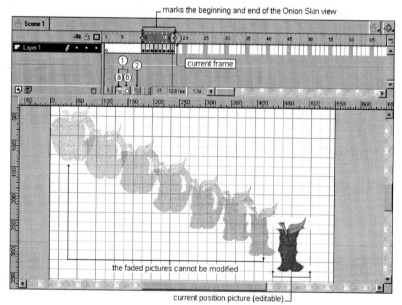

marks the beginning and end of the Onion Skin view

current frame

the faded pictures cannot be modified

current position picture (editable)

① Activate the **Onion Skin** button (a) to show all the pictures in the movie. Only the image that corresponds to the current position appears in full colour, the others are faded to make them transparent. Activate the **Onion Skin Outlines** button (b) if you only want to show the borders of the pictures.

② By default, Flash will only allow you to change one image at a time, which is the image that corresponds to the current position (of the playhead), but if you want to edit the others without having to activate the corresponding frames, click the **Edit Multiple Frames** button. All the images between the start and end markers appear in full colour and can be individually edited.

Setting the Onion Skin view markers

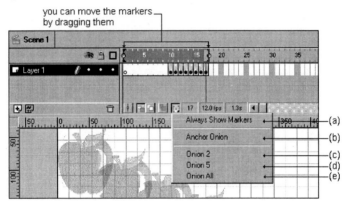

you can move the markers by dragging them

░ Click the **Modify Onion Markers** button then choose an option:

(a)   to show the Onion Skin view markers in the Timeline border, whether the **Onion Skin** or **Onion Skin Outlines** buttons are active or not.

(b)   to lock the markers in their current position.

(c)   to show two images on either side of the current image.

(d)   to show five images on either side of the current image.

(e)   to show all the images on either side of the current image.

⇨ *To make your screen more legible, you can lock or hide layers that you do not want to see the Onion Skins for. When you are in Onion Skin mode, locked layers are hidden.*

G-Editing a frame or keyframe

Redoing the image in a keyframe

░ Select the keyframe concerned in the **Timeline** window and use **Insert - Clear Keyframe** or ⇧ Shift F6 .

The keyframe and its contents are deleted and replaced by a frame containing a copy of the contents of the preceding keyframe.

MAKING MOVIES

Inserting a new frame into a movie

- In the Timeline window, click the frame that should precede the new one.
- **Insert - Frame** or F5

Inserting a new blank keyframe into a movie

- In the Timeline window, click the frame that should precede the new keyframe.
- **Insert - Blank Keyframe** or F7

Deleting one or more frames

- In the Timeline window, click the frame you want to delete, or select the frames by dragging.
- Right-click the selection and choose the **Delete Frame** option in the context menu, or press ⇧ Shift F5.

Deleting one or more keyframes

- In the Timeline window, click the keyframe you want to delete, or select the keyframes by dragging.
- Right-click the selection and choose **Clear Keyframe** from the context menu, or press ⇧ Shift F6.

Moving a frame by frame animation

- Click the **Edit Multiple Frames** button.
- Click the **Modify Onion Markers** button and activate the **Onion All** option.
- **Edit - Select All**
- Drag the whole sequence to its new position in the scene.

4.2 Tweened animation

Unlike frame by frame movies, for which Flash must save all the information for each frame, using tweened animation means that Flash only saves the values of the changes between the beginning and end frames. This type of animation is therefore much more compact.

A-Creating a movie using shape tweening

If you want to give the impression that Flash 4 has turned one shape into another, you need to create an animation using shape tweening. Shape tweening can be applied to the position, size and also colour of a shape. While Flash is able to interpolate as many shapes as you like on a layer, you will achieve the best results if you use just one shape on a layer.

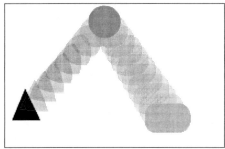

Here are two examples of shape tweening. The triangle changes into a circle, and the circle into a rectangle with rounded corners.

▓ Activate (or create) an empty layer and make sure that the playhead is placed over a blank keyframe. This is the starting point of the shape tweening animation.

▓ Create the object that will be the first image in the sequence using Flash's drawing tools (see 2.1 - Graphic tools).

▓ When you have created an object you are happy with, click the current frame in the Timeline.

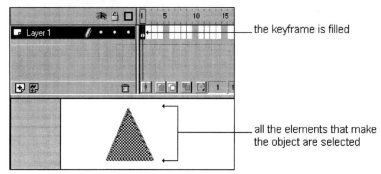

the keyframe is filled

all the elements that make the object are selected

▓ Double-click the current frame in the Timeline.

MAKING MOVIES

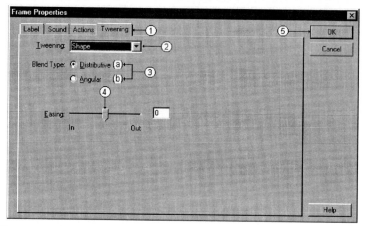

① Activate this tab if need be.

② Open this list and choose the **Shape** option.

③ Activate the option:

    (a)   to make the intermediate shapes more rounded and regular.

    (b)   to keep the corners and straight lines distinctive in the intermediate shapes.

④ Set the speed of the animation's transition by dragging the cursor. By default, the cursor is placed in the middle for a regular rate of change between tweened shapes. If you move the cursor to the left (**In**), the image will be changed slowly at the beginning, speeding up towards the end.

⑤ Confirm the properties of the current frame.

▨ In the Timeline, click the cell where you want to stop the shape tween, and press ⌨F6 or use **Insert - Keyframe**.

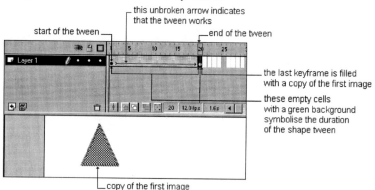

At this stage, there are two identical, static images. One is situated at the start of the tween and the other at the end. The next step consists of deleting the image in the last keyframe (the copy) and replacing it with a new shape.

- If necessary, select the image of the last keyframe on the stage, and press ⌊Del⌋ or use **Edit - Clear**.

  Notice that, in the Timeline window, a blank keyframe replaces the last keyframe.

- Create the new target object where you want to on the stage using the drawing tools.

- Test your shape tweening animation by pressing ⌊Enter⌋ or by **Control - Play**.

Flash 4 progressively transforms the first image to obtain the shape of the end image in the defined position.

Inserting a new keyframe into a shape tween

You can insert one (or more) new keyframes into a shape tween if you want to insert a specific shape between the start and the end of the animation.

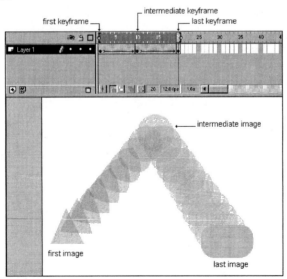

Here is an example of an insertion of an intermediate keyframe to separate the original tween into two stages.

- In the Timeline, click the cell in which you want to insert the new keyframe and press ⌊F6⌋.

- Press ⌊Del⌋ to remove the object selected on the stage.

- Create the new intermediate image where you want on the stage.

MAKING MOVIES

▓ Test the animation by pressing ⌨️Enter.

When a shape tween does not work

If you have used a text block, a bitmap image, a symbol or a group of objects, the tween will not work, or will work incorrectly.

▓ If you have used a group or a symbol as the last image in the sequence, the arrow that symbolises the tween in the Timeline window looks correct (is unbroken). However, when you test the animation, there is no interpolation between the beginning and the end of the animation. To interpolate a group or a symbol, you need to break it down into its constituent parts: on the stage, select the group or symbol concerned, and use **Modify - Break Apart** (or ⌨️Ctrl **B**).

▓ To use a group or a symbol as the first image in the sequence, break it down to its constituent parts <u>before</u> generating the shape tween.

⇨ *You cannot create a shape tween using a text block or a bitmap image. If you try to, Flash signals that there is a problem by replacing the arrow in the Timeline with a dashed line.*

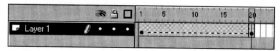

B-Creating a movie using motion tweening

During a motion tween, Flash allows you to change the direction, size, orientation, colour and brightness of various objects in a layer. However, you can only apply one effect to all the objects in the layer (and this must be the same effect for all the objects). This means that it is impossible to generate several motion tweens for different objects in the same layer, except movie clip symbols, because these are independent animations that are on the stage as instances. The instance itself can be interpolated.

So that this sort of tweening works correctly, you should define any objects as symbols. In fact, only instances of symbols can be animated by interpolation.

▓ Create a new layer if you want to apply a motion tween to a new object which has not yet been animated or inserted as an image. If not, click the name of the layer you want to use.

▓ In the Timeline, click the blank keyframe that corresponds to the beginning of the animation.

- To create the object, you can:
  - use Flash's drawing tools to draw it,
  - drag an instance of a symbol from the Library (see 3.2 - E: Creating and managing an instance of a symbol),
  - import a graphic (see Importing a file).
- Once the object is where you want it to be and has the required appearance, select it using the **Arrow** tool, and use **Insert - Create Motion Tween**.

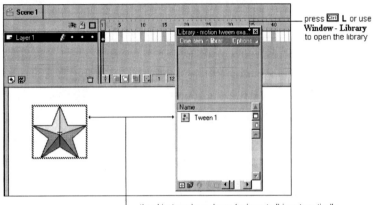

press **Ctrl** **L** or use
Window - **Library**
to open the library

the object you have drawn (or imported) is automatically
converted into a symbol and placed in the Library under **Tween x**

- In the Timeline, click the cell that is to be the last frame in the animation. If there is no frame in this cell, use **Insert - Frame** or press **F5**.

The motion tween you are creating is, for the moment, indicated in the Timeline by a dashed line between the first frame and the end frame.

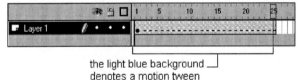

the light blue background ⌐
denotes a motion tween

- Move the object on the stage to the end point of the animation by dragging it.

Flash instantly inserts a keyframe and transforms the dashed line in the Timeline into an unbroken arrow. The motion tween has been created.

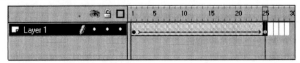

In this example, the motion tween that has been created is basic, but it can be modified to include more sophisticated effects (see 4.2 - C - Managing motion tween properties).

MAKING MOVIES

C-Managing motion tween properties

Viewing a motion tween's settings

░ Double-click the end keyframe of the motion tween.

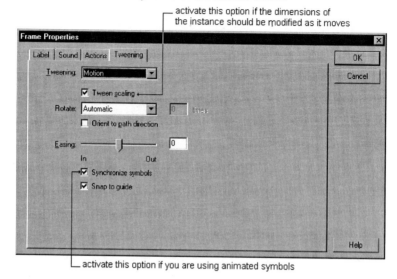

— activate this option if the dimensions of the instance should be modified as it moves

— activate this option if you are using animated symbols

Rotating an object along a path

░ In the Timeline, drag to select all the cells that correspond to the path along which the object is to rotate.

░ **Modify - Frame** or Ctrl **F**

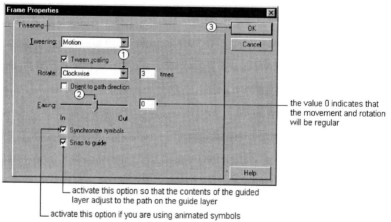

— the value 0 indicates that the movement and rotation will be regular

— activate this option so that the contents of the guided layer adjust to the path on the guide layer

— activate this option if you are using animated symbols

① Open the list associated with the **Rotate** box and choose an option:

None if you want Flash 4 to cancel the rotation.

Automatic if you have already rotated the instance between the first and end points using **Modify - Transform - Rotate**. In this case, Flash 4 calculates and chooses the most simple rotation available.

Clockwise or **Counterclockwise** to rotate the object on its axis until it reaches its new position. If the rotation should be repeated, indicate the number of **times** in the corresponding text box. The value **0** deactivates any tweened rotation.

② Drag the cursor along the ruler to change the speed of the rotation and movement of the object. Move the cursor to the left (**In**) to start the object moving slowly then increase its speed, or to the right (**Out**) to slow the object as it reaches the end.

③ Confirm your settings.

Creating a motion tween that follows a guide

If you want to make an animation of an instance, group, or text block follow a particular path, you can use a motion guide layer in which you can draw the path. By linking this guide layer to the layers that contain the elements you want to animate, several objects will follow the same path. A normal layer that is linked to a motion guide layer becomes a guided layer.

▓ In the Timeline, select the normal layer for which you want to create a guide.

▓ **Insert - Motion Guide**

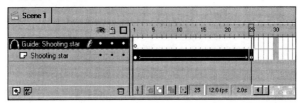

Flash 4 adds a Guide layer to the active layer. Notice that the new layer carries the name of the layer to which it is linked.

▓ In the Timeline, click the blank keyframe in the new guide layer.

▓ Using the **Pencil, Line, Circle, Rectangle** or **Brush** tools, draw the path you want the motion tween to follow on the stage.

MAKING MOVIES

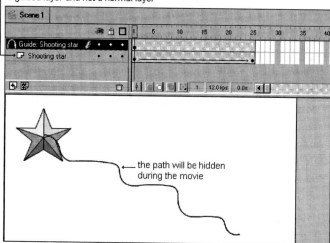

the slight indent here shows that this is a guided layer and not a normal layer

the path will be hidden during the movie

▦ To adjust the centre of the first and last images in the motion tween to the start and end of the guide, select the first or last keyframe of the guided layer in the Timeline, select the corresponding image on the stage, and drag it so that it is aligned to the beginning or end of the path.

▦ Test the animation by clicking, in the Timeline, in the first keyframe in the guide layer or the guided layer then press ⌷Enter⌷.

If you want to hide the guide so that it is not visible when the movie is playing, click in the eye column at the level of the corresponding guide.

⇨ *The contents of the guided layer are adjusted according to the path in the guide layer if the **Snap to guide** option is active in the **Frame Properties** dialog box. If the guide controls not only the movement but also the direction, activate the **Orient to path direction** option (see 4.2 - C - Viewing a motion tween's settings).*

Linking a normal layer to a motion guide layer

▦ In the Timeline, drag the layer in question to under the motion guide layer.

The normal layer becomes a guided layer and is slightly indented to the right; all the objects in this layer are adjusted to the path in the motion guide layer. A link has been established between the layers.

Disassociating a guided layer from a motion guide layer

▦ In the Timeline window, click the name of the guided layer in question to select it.

▦ Drag the selected guided layer above the motion guide layer or use **Modify - Layer** and activate the **Normal** option.

4.3 Movie clips

A-Discovering movie clips

▨ An animated sequence can be saved as a movie clip symbol so that you can reuse it as an instance in another animation.

▨ This animated sequence is controlled in a specific Timeline window.

B-Converting a movie into a movie clip

Flash 4 allows you to convert an animated sequence created in a scene into a movie clip symbol, so that you can reuse it later in the movie or so that you can use it as an instance.

▨ Select all the frames in each animated layer.

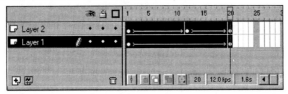

In this example, the movie is composed of two layers, each containing twenty frames.

▨ **Edit - Copy Frame** or `Ctrl` `Alt` **C**

▨ Make sure that there is no active selection on the stage and use **Insert - New Symbol** or `Ctrl` `F8`.

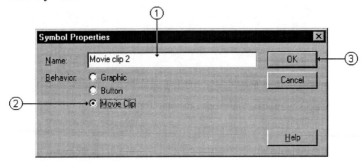

① Enter the name of the symbol.

② Activate this option.

③ Confirm.

Flash 4 opens the scene again so that you can edit the movie clip.

▨ Click the first keyframe in the Timeline window and use **Edit - Paste Frames** or `Ctrl` `Alt` **V**.

Flash 4 pastes the frames you copied previously into the new clip.

MAKING MOVIES

- Close the symbol editing window and return to the stage using **Edit - Edit Movie**.

- You can now remove the animation from the main movie Timeline by selecting all the frames in each layer of the animation and using **Insert - Delete Frame** or ⧏ Shift⧐ ⧏F5⧐.

- To use a movie clip, drag it from the Library onto the stage as with any other symbol instance.

⇨ *To read movie clips in the Library, use the buttons in the top right hand corner of the clip preview. You cannot read clips directly in the scene. To read them you need to use **Test Scene** from the **Control** menu to animate them.*

4.4 Masks

A-Discovering the Mask layer

The Mask layer is a tool that enables you to create highlighting and transitional effects. The principle consists of placing a Mask layer over another layer in order to hide its instances, except in the area where you place a filled object, which creates a hole that allows you to see the layer below. The filled object can only be a shape, an instance or a single text object.

Here is an example of a Mask layer:

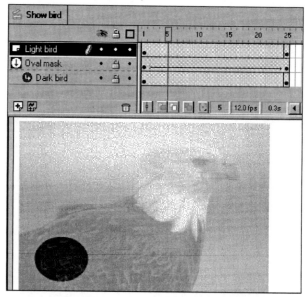

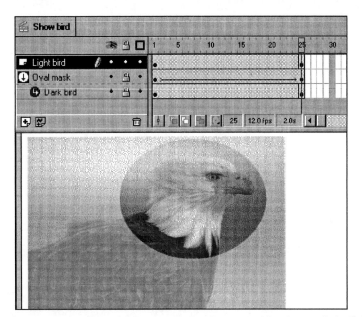

In this example, the oval is moved and increased in size until the bird's head is visible. Outside of the oval area, the mask completely hides the layer underneath. The "light" picture of the bird is, in fact, a copy of the background image which has been lightened and placed on a foreground layer.

This example was created following this principle:

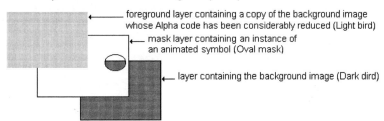

foreground layer containing a copy of the background image whose Alpha code has been considerably reduced (Light bird)

mask layer containing an instance of an animated symbol (Oval mask)

layer containing the background image (Dark dird)

Several mask layers can be grouped in the same layer in order to create complicated effects. A mask layer can contain all types of animation, except a motion path (guide). You should also be aware that a mask cannot be used over buttons.

B-Creating a Mask layer

Create an ordinary layer whose contents will be visible through "holes" in the Mask layer.

If necessary, select the layer and use **Insert - Layer**.

MAKING MOVIES

For the moment this new layer is a normal layer but it will later be transformed into a Mask layer; it is important to make sure that it is placed just above the layer it is supposed to hide.

▨ Draw a filled shape in this new layer, which can be a geometric shape, text, or an instance of a symbol. The colour you choose is of no importance because all filled surfaces will be transparent when the movie plays, and the unfilled areas will be opaque.

▨ If you like, animate the object in the future mask, just as you would animate any instance using motion tweening.

▨ In the Timeline, right-click the name of the layer you want to make into a mask and choose the **Mask** command from the context menu to turn this normal layer into a Mask layer.

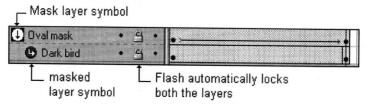

In this example, a motion tween animation has been created in the Mask layer.

C-Managing a Mask layer

Modifying a Mask or masked layer

▨ Unlock the layer concerned by clicking the little padlock in the Timeline, which deactivates the mask. To reactivate the mask, lock one of the layers again.

Linking an existing layer to a Mask

▨ Drag to move the layer in question under the Mask layer. You can associate several layers with a Mask layer.

The layer you have moved is slightly indented under the Mask layer and its symbol changes.

Linking a new layer to a Mask

▨ Insert a new layer under the Mask layer using the **Insert - Layer** command.

▨ Select it, then choose **Masked** as its type in the **Layer Properties** dialog box, which you can open by **Modify - Layer**.

Disassociating layers from a Mask layer

▨ Select the layer you want to disassociate and drag it above the Mask layer. You can also use **Modify - Layer** and choose the **Normal** option.

4.5 Scenes

A-Overview

A scene is in fact an extract of a movie. A movie can contain several scenes. When you play a Flash movie that contains several scenes, they are played in the order in which they are listed in the Scene Inspector (Window - Inspectors - Scene).

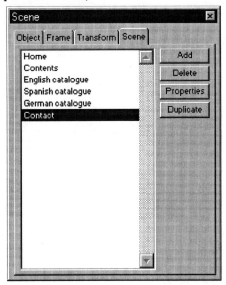

You can intervene in the way the scenes play by assigning actions to images (see 5.1 - Interactive movies). In this way you can, for example, stop the movie playing at the end of each scene, or let the user choose how to play the movie.

B-Managing scenes

▓ To open a particular scene, use **View - Goto** or click the **Edit Scene** button ▦ then click the name of the scene you want to see.

▓ To add a scene, use **Insert - Scene** or click the **Add** button in the Scene Inspector window.

Flash inserts a new scene in the Scene Inspector window after the active scene.

▓ You can delete a scene by selecting it and using **Insert - Remove Scene**, or by selecting it in the Scene Inspector and clicking the **Delete** button.

All the objects in the scene's layers are deleted at the same time. You can still find them in the Library if they were converted to symbols.
If the movie contains only one scene, you cannot delete it.

- Rename a scene by selecting it in the Scene Inspector and clicking the **Properties** button. Type the new name then click **OK** to confirm. You can also open the scene and use **Modify - Scene**.

- To copy a scene, select it in the Scene Inspector and click the **Duplicate** button.

  Flash creates a new scene with the same name as the source scene, followed by "copy".

- You can change the position of a scene in the movie by selecting its name in the Scene Inspector and dragging it to its new position.

C-Playing scenes

Playing the active scene

- To show the controller in a new window, use **Window - Controller**.

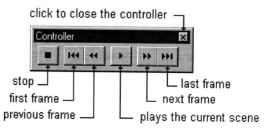

click to close the controller

stop — first frame — previous frame — plays the current scene — next frame — last frame

The movie sequence is played in the workscreen.

⇨ *You can also use the Play command in the Control menu, or press Enter to play the active scene.*

Playing the active scene in a loop

- Activate the **Loop Playback** option in the **Control** menu.
- Start playing the scene, using whatever method you like.
- To stop playing the scene, click a frame in the Timeline.
- If necessary, deactivate the **Loop Playback** command in the **Control** menu.

Playing all the scenes in a movie

- Activate the **Play All Scenes** command in the **Control** menu.
- Start playing the current scene.
- If necessary, deactivate the **Play All Scenes** option in the **Control** menu.

Playing a movie with the sound turned off

- Activate the **Mute Sounds** command in the **Control** menu, or press Ctrl Alt **M**.
- Start playing the active scene, using whatever method you like.

4.6 Sounds

A-Using sound in Flash 4

▓ Flash 4 is not destined for the creation of sounds, but you do have the possibility of integrating sounds into your movies.

▓ Flash 4 supports two main types of sound:

- **Stream sounds**, which, for example, allow you to play background music throughout a movie. Stream sound is mostly used as a background sound. This type of sound is placed on one of the layers of the movie as an object. It begins to play as soon as part of the sound has been downloaded. As the start of the sound sequence plays, the next part is downloaded and so on. The sound is played for as long as its layer is active in the Timeline. It will be interrupted if, for example, the scene changes.

- **Event sounds** are sounds that play when, for example, a particular button is clicked, making your movie more interactive. An event sound is principally destined at emphasising the actions on interactive objects. It is best to use short sounds as event sounds, because the whole file must be downloaded before the sound will play.

▓ Audio files tend to require a lot of disk space, which means that the files that need to be downloaded to play your movie will increase considerably. You should therefore use sound sparingly in your movies.

▓ Flash 4 recommends 22 kHz, 16 bit mono sounds (stereo sound uses twice as much space as mono sound). You can use 8 and 16 bit samples in Flash 4, at a sampling rate of 11, 22 or 44 kHz. Once a sound file has been loaded, you can resample it with Flash 4.

B-Importing a wave sound

Flash 4 only uses .wav format files for background sound. You cannot import midi or MP3 files into Flash 4, nor can you import other music formats. The process of importing a sound file is similar to that for an external animation object.

▓ **File - Import** or Ctrl R

▓ Select the .wav format file you want to import, and click **Open**.

MAKING MOVIES

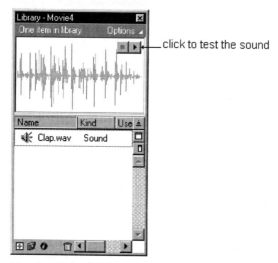

click to test the sound

The sound is placed in the Library as a symbol straight away, and can now be placed in a movie as an instance.

⇨ *Although it is recommended you use 16 bit sounds, try to use short audio files or 8 bit sounds rather than 16 bits if your computer does not have very much RAM.*

C-Inserting a sound into a movie

▓ Create a new layer in the movie in question using **Insert - Layer**.

To make it easier to test and manage your audio data, use a different layer for each sound file.

▓ In the Timeline, click the keyframe where you want to start playing the sound.

▓ To create an instance of a sound and define its settings, use **Modify - Frame** or Ctrl **F**.

characteristics of the selected file

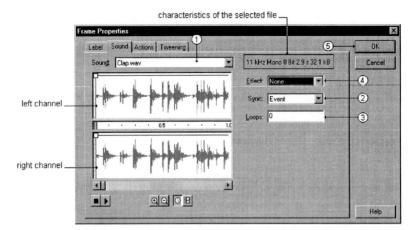

① Open this list and select the name of the audio file that corresponds to the sound you want to use. This list contains all the "sound" symbols in the Library.

② Define the synchronisation by choosing one of the four choices:

Event to synchronise the sound file with an event. The sound will be played when its keyframe appears for the first time. The length of time it plays is independent of the Timeline, even if the movie is interrupted.

Start to play the sound when the keyframe plays, in which case, the sound has the same behaviour as with an Event synchronisation.

Stop to interrupt the sound.

Stream to synchronise the sound for Web use. In this case, the movie and the stream sounds should play at the same pace, which means that Flash forces the movie to keep pace with the sound. If several stream sound layers have been defined, the sounds are mixed in the movie. Unlike an Event sound, stream sounds stop when the movie stops. This means that a stream sound cannot be longer than the frames it accompanies.

③ Enter the number of times the sound should loop. If you want the sound to play continuously, enter a high number.

④ Define the sound instance's settings using these options:

None the sound will be played as it was imported. This option also allows you to remove any previously defined audio settings.

Left or **Right Channel** the sound will only be played through the chosen channel.

MAKING MOVIES

Fade Left to Right or Fade Right to Left	the sound will be sent from one channel to the other.
Fade In	the sound will gradually become louder as it plays.
Fade Out	the sound will gradually become quieter as it plays.
Custom	you can define the sound settings by directly modifying its profile in the window using the envelope handles.

⑤ Confirm.

⇨ *To insert a sound into a layer, you can also activate the keyframe concerned by the sound in the Timeline, and then drag an instance of the sound from the Library. The sound does not appear but a keyframe is created. Double-click the keyframe to define the sound settings in the* **Sound** *tab of the* **Frame Properties** *dialog box.*

D-Associating a sound with a button

You can associate sounds to a button's every status. The sounds are stored with the button, and so are linked to every instance of the button.

▓ Create a new button or select an existing button in the Library.

▓ Open the **Options** list in the Library and choose **Modify**.

Flash switches to symbol editing mode.

▓ In the button's Timeline, add a layer.

▓ In the new audio layer, create a keyframe for each status. For example, if the sound is to play when a user clicks the button, create a keyframe in the **Down** frame.

▓ Add a sound to the new keyframe and choose an **Event** synchronisation.

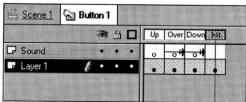

▓ Return to the current scene by closing symbol editing mode (**Edit - Edit Movie** or Ctrl **E**).

⇨ *You can associate a different sound with each of the button's keyframes by using a different audio layer for each keyframe. The sound file used can be different for each keyframe if you want, but you can use the same sound file and create or use a different audio effect for each of the button's keyframes.*

E-Controlling the sound

▓ In the Timeline, select a frame that contains the sound.

▓ Use **Modify - Frame** and activate the **Sound** tab in the **Frame Properties** dialog box.

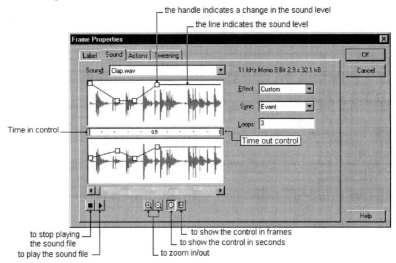

the handle indicates a change in the sound level

the line indicates the sound level

Time in control

Time out control

to stop playing the sound file

to play the sound file

to show the control in frames

to show the control in seconds

to zoom in/out

▓ To change the sound's start and finish points, drag the **Time In Control** and the **Time Out Control** on the ruler.

The ruler can display either the number of seconds the sound plays for, or the frame position in the Timeline.

▓ Drag a handle on the line to change the sound level at different points in the sound.

▓ To create a handle, click the line.

▓ Delete a handle by dragging it out of the window.

⇨ *The **Sound** page of the **Frame Properties** dialog box is always composed of two parts, whether the sound is in mono or stereo.*

F-Synchronising a sound and a movie

▓ When you want a sound to play and stop in synchronisation with a movie, create a layer in which you need to tell Flash when to play the sound. The play/stop order will thus be in the same sound layer.

▓ Choose the first keyframe that corresponds to the event keyframe in the scene, and add a sound.

▓ Create a keyframe in the sound layer in the frame where the sound is to stop playing.

Notice that a representation of the sound file appears in the Timeline header.

▓ Double-click the keyframe to open the **Frame Properties** dialog box.

MAKING MOVIES

- In the **Sound** list, choose the same sound as that used at the beginning of the sound sequence.
- Open the **Sync** drop-down list and choose **Stop**.
- Click **OK** to confirm your choices and close the **Frame Properties** dialog box.

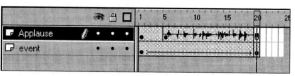

In this example, the sound sequence starts in the fifth frame of the motion tween animation and finishes in the same frame.

⇨ *Hold the* [⇧ Shift] *key down and drag the playhead along the Timeline header so that Flash repeats the stream sound from the active frame.*

G-Compressing a sound file

Before exporting a sound movie (see 6.2 - Exporting and publishing), you must control the quality and size of each sound. In fact, the sampling rate and degree of compression of a sound file are very important. Flash can offer you four different methods for compressing sound files.

- Right-click the sound file concerned in the Library and choose the **Properties** command from the context menu.
- Using the options in the **Export Settings** frame, define the **Compression** settings.

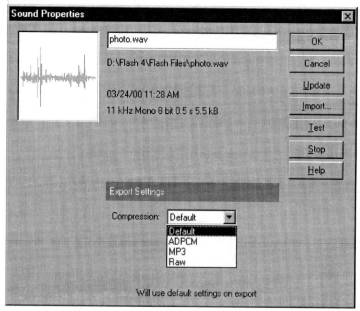

Standard compression

▓ The **Default** compression uses Flash's publication settings (**File - Publish Settings**). If you choose this option, there are no additional options available to define the compression settings.

ADPCM compression

This option sets the compression for 16 bit sound files. This type of compression is for short event sounds, such as a sound that accompanies a button-click.

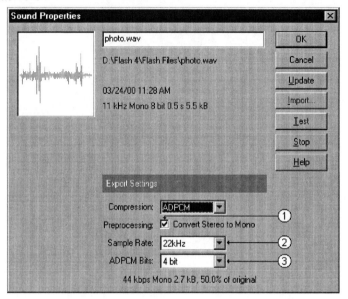

① Activate this option if you want to convert a stereo sound to mono. This will mean 50% less data. If the sound is already in mono, there will be no change.

② Choose one of the four sample rates. The higher the rate, the better the sound quality and the larger file size. Remember that 44 kHz corresponds to the standard audio CD rate. For sounds that will be broadcast on the Internet, 22 kHz is quite sufficient for music, and voices remain comprehensible at 5 kHz. Flash 4 cannot improve the sound, so there is no point in choosing a higher sample rate than the original one. The audio quality will not be improved and the amount of data will increase.

③ Define the number of bits used by ADPCM coding. The lower this number is, the poorer the sound quality, but the compression is greater.

MP3 compression

MP3 is one of the three audiovisual data compression levels developed by the Moving Pictures Expert Group. The MPEG Layer 3 or MP3 process is for audio data, and can compress data to one twelfth of their original size. This type of compression is very useful for long stream sounds.

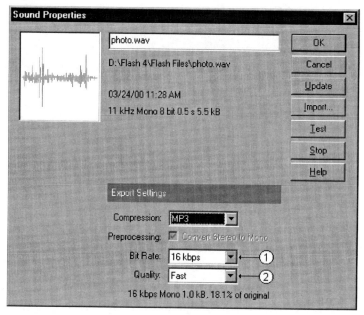

① Define the maximum rate (in kbps) of sound produced by the MP3 encoder. This figure should be at least 16 kbps. The more precision you require, the higher this value should be. A dynamic sound will require a rate of 48 kbps, and classical music requires an even higher rate.

② Define the quality of the compression. The **Fast** option is ideal for Internet use.

⇨ As MP3 is a very compact audio format, use it as much as possible.

Raw compression

This compression option allows you to export sounds without compressing them.

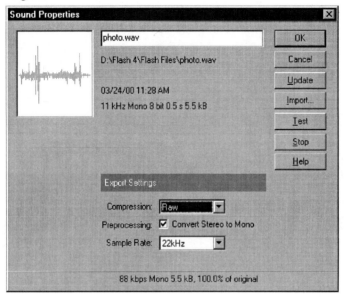

5.1 Interactive movies

A-Overview

▓ Unlike **static animations**, in which the frames of the scene are played one after the other in the order defined in the Scenes Inspector, an **interactive movie** takes the user into account. This means that a user can intervene on how the scenes play or answer questions using the mouse or keyboard. His or her choices will then affect the way the movie plays.

▓ The basic principle of interactivity in a movie consists of starting an <u>action</u> when an <u>event</u> happens. The action might be to start a program or show an image, and is associated with a keyframe using programming statements. The statements (instructions) used in the program can be summarised in one action (stopping the movie, for example) or they might also correspond to several nested actions (such as evaluating data before starting another action).

▓ If you want to create very elaborate Flash movies using complex actions, you must have a good knowledge of programming languages. However, you can still create interactive movies using the several predefined actions, which do not require much programming experience. The actions that require familiarity with programming languages will not be dealt with in this book.

B-Associating an action with a frame

In order to give you an idea of how to program an action, two instructions, Go To and Load Movie, will be looked at here.
Remember that an action starts when Flash 4 reaches the corresponding keyframe. You should place frame actions in separate layers.

▓ If necessary, insert a new layer using **Insert - Layer**.

▓ In the Timeline, select the keyframe concerned and open the **Frame Properties** window using **Modify - Frame** or by double-click the keyframe.

▓ Activate the **Actions** tab.

▓ Click the [+] button to see the list of available statements.

Each statement corresponds to a specific action.

Statement	Action
Go To	goes to a particular frame or scene in the movie.
Play	starts the movie.
Stop	stops the movie.
Toggle High Quality	activates or deactivates antialiasing (prevents pixelisation in the movie).
Stop All Sounds	stops the audio track without stopping the movie.
Get URL	goes to a URL to find a document.
FS Command	is used to send a message to Flash Player's host program.
Load/Unload Movie	is used to run or deletes supplementary movies without closing Flash Player.
Tell Target	is used to control a movie clip (linked to Load Movie).
If Frame is Loaded	is used to define a specific number of frames in an introduction.
On MouseEvent	inserts On/End On instructions.
If	is used to define the running conditions.
Loop	is used to define a series of instructions that will run repeatedly as long as a specific condition is met.
Call	is used to run the same action as a given button, without having to copy it.
Set Variable	is used to attribute a value to a variable.
Duplicate/ Remove Movie Clip	is used to create or cancel an instance of a movie clip.
Drag Movie Clip	is used to move a movie clip.
Trace	is used to display information in an output window
Comment	is used to add notes to an image or button action.

▓ Click the statements you want to use.

Each statement has its own settings. The programming interface (also called the Parameters pane) in the right of the dialog box changes depending on the instruction you choose.

1st example: Go To statement

In this example, the Go To statement is used to go to a particular frame or scene in the movie. This statement's default behaviour involves going directly to a frame and stopping the movie, but you can also start playing another scene from this frame.

░ Define the settings for the action you have chosen using the lists of options available in the programming interface, or by directly entering a program code in the appropriate text boxes.

delete the selected statement ─── move the selected statement up or down

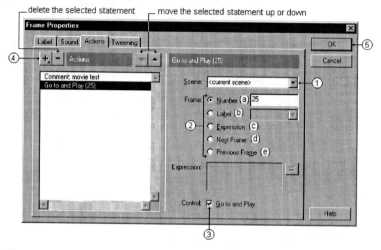

① In the drop-down list of the scenes in the movie, select the one to which you want to go (Flash suggests the current scene by default).

② To go to a particular **Frame**, activate one of these options:

(a)   and type the frame number.

(b)   and select the name of the frame you want in the drop-down list (see 5.1 - C - Labelling a keyframe).

(c)   and enter the program code in the **Expression** frame.

(d)   to go to the frame that follows the keyframe you are programming.

(e)   to go to the frame that precedes the keyframe you are programming.

③ If necessary, activate this option to tell the movie to play from the specified frame. If this option is not active, the movie stops at the specified frame.

④ If necessary, add a new action that will run after the one you have already defined, and choose its settings in the programming interface.

⑤ Once all the actions have been inserted and set, save them in the movie.

2nd example: Load/Unload Movie statement

*This is another basic action that does not require you to be familiar with programming languages, which can be very useful. In fact, the **Load Movie** statement allows you load external movies, simultaneously if you like, and, inversely, the **Unload Movie** statement unloads these movies when they are no longer necessary.*

In any case, be careful when you are using these statements because loading movies has a marked effect on the speed of your movie. A movie

*that is loaded but not playing on the screen is nevertheless played in the background, which makes it all the more prudent to unload it using **Unload Movie**.*

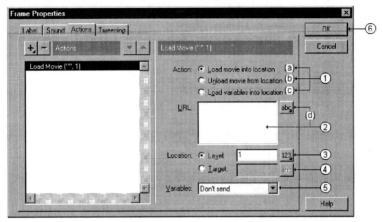

① Choose the action you want to use by activating one of these options:

    (a)   to load a movie in the current movie.

    (b)   to unload a movie. Notice that the statement shown in the left of the dialog box becomes **Unload Movie** rather than **Load Movie**.

    (c)   to load a variable from a remote text file. Notice that the statement on the left of the dialog box becomes **Load Variables**.

② Type the URL address of the movie that is to be loaded. The addressing can be relative or absolute thanks to the options on button (d). If you are testing your project locally, all the movies need to be in the same folder on your computer.

③ Indicate the layer or the target of the **Load Movie** or **Unload Movie** instruction. In Flash Player, movie files are numbered chronologically according to the order in which they are loaded. Level 0 corresponds to the movie that is loaded first, meaning the lowest layer. The debit, background colour and format of all the other movies that are loaded are defined according to the movie on layer 0. The other movies are stacked on higher layers, above layer 0.

④ If necessary, define the movie that will replace the loaded movie. In this case, the loaded movie will receive the position, rotation and dimensions of the target movie.

⑤ Specify that you want to send preset variables for a loaded movie to the location given as a URL. This means that you can send variables to a CGI script that generates a SWF file as a CGI output. To do this, choose the **Send using GET** or **Send using POST** method, depending on the contents of the URL that is to be loaded or to which the variable is to be sent.

⑥ Once all the actions have been inserted and their settings defined, save them in the movie.

After you confirm the action programming, the frame associated with the actions is indicated by a small a in the Timeline.

⇨ *To change the settings of an existing action, double-click the keyframe concerned to see its properties, click the action you want to edit in the **Actions** tab, and enter or choose the new values in the programming interface.*

⇨ *To test the loading of variables, use **File - Publish Preview**. You need an active network connection to do this.*

⇨ *To test a frame action in a scene, use **Control - Enable Frame Actions** or* ⌷Ctrl⌷⌷Alt⌷ ***A** before playing the movie.*

C-Labelling a keyframe

Flash allows you to label keyframes, meaning name them. This can be useful for programming purposes: rather than referring to the number of the keyframe, it is easier to identify them using their names.

▦ To label a keyframe, select it in the Timeline and use **Modify - Frame** or ⌷Ctrl⌷ **F**.

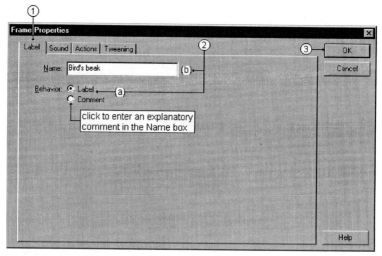

① Activate this tab.

② Activate option (a) then type the name you want to give the keyframe (b).

③ Confirm this information.

*The text entered as **Label** or **Comment** appears in the Timeline, which makes it easier to identify keyframes.*

▓ To use a keyframe's label rather than its number when you are programming, open the list associated with the **Label** option in the programming interface and select the name you want:

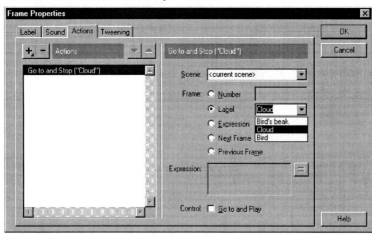

⇨ *Be careful, Flash does not control the labels you give to keyframes, so several keyframes can have the same label, making programming errors likely.*

5.2 Buttons

A-Discovering buttons

A button is a type of symbol with which several frames are associated. These frames, often different, are activated by different mouse events. The button symbol interacts with mouse actions.

▓ Creating a button consists of creating a button-type symbol and, in a specific Timeline window, defining different keyframes for each different state. The Timeline window of a button symbol contains four predefined frames that correspond to the four possible states of a button.

(a) (b) (c) (d)

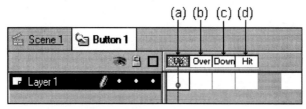

(a)   the **Up** state contains a picture of the button as it should appear when the mouse pointer is nowhere near it.

(b)   the **Over** state contains a picture of the button as it should appear when the mouse pointer is over it.

(c)   the **Down** state contains a picture of the button as it should appear when a user clicks it.

(d)   the **Hit** state defines the sensitive area of the button, on which a click can produce a particular action. There is no frame associated with this state. The hotspot defined here is invisible in the movie.

▨ When the button symbol has been created and its different states defined, you can make it interactive by associating an action with the button.

B-Creating a button symbol

▨ Make sure that nothing is selected on the stage.

▨ **Insert - New Symbol** or Ctrl F8

▨ Enter the **Name** of the button in the **Symbol Properties** window.

▨ Activate the **Button** option in the **Behavior** list then click **OK**.

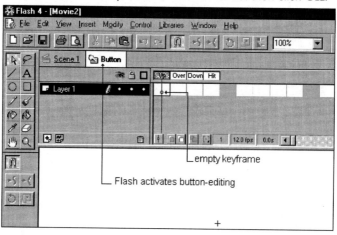

Apart from the four predefined cells Up, Over, Down and Hit, the other cells in the Timeline have no purpose.

▨ Create the keyframe for the **Up** state on the stage, either by using the drawing tools or by importing a graphic, or even by using an instance of another symbol from the Library. In this last case, you can use a graphic or movie clip symbol, but not a button symbol.

To create an animated button, use a Movie Clip symbol.

▨ Click the blank frame corresponding to the **Over** state, and use **Insert - Keyframe** or F6.

A picture of the button in the first frame is copied onto the stage.

▨ Change the aspect of the button in the **Over** state.

- Click the blank frame that corresponds to the **Down** state and use **Insert - Keyframe** or F6.
- Change the aspect of the button in the **Down** state.
- To define a **Hit** keyframe, activate the blank frame in question and use **Insert - Keyframe** or F6.

Remember that when a movie is played, the Hit frame is not visible on the stage, but corresponds to the button's hotspot that reacts to a click.

The graphic of the Hit frame needs to be large enough to cover all the graphic elements of the Up, Over, and Down states. The zone in question can be larger than the button.

- To create a **Hit** image, you can draw a rectangle (or another shape) which is larger than the space used by the image of the visible button.

If you do not create a Hit keyframe, Flash uses the objects in the Up state as the default hotspot.

- To leave button-editing mode and return to the current scene, use **Edit - Edit Movie**.
- To use the button symbol you have just created, drag it from the Library onto the stage to create an instance.

⇨ *You can assign a sound to a button's states (see 4.6 - D - Associating a sound with a button).*

C-Assigning an action to a button

If you want users to be free to move around in your movie and to carry out operations, you can associate an action to an instance of a button so that this action runs when the user clicks the button or drags the mouse pointer across it.

Note that when you assign an action to a particular instance of a button, this has no effect on the other instances of the button.

The action associated with an instance of a button can be started by an event which is linked to the mouse (click or drag, for example) or by a key on the keyboard.

- Select the button instance in question and use **Modify - Instance** or double-click the instance.
- Activate the **Actions** tab.

If the Actions tab is not available, the selected instance is not a button.

- Click the ⊞ button to see a list of available statements.

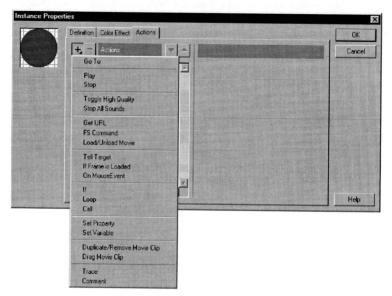

Click the statement of your choice.

*Flash completes the chosen statement with two complementary statements: **On** and **End On**. These statements correspond to the **On MouseEvent** action.*

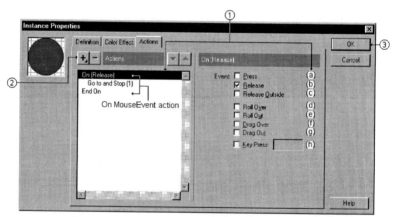

*In this example, the **Go To** action has been chosen and Flash has automatically added the **On MouseEvent** action.*

① Click the **On (Release)** instruction to edit the mouse and keyboard events that trigger the action:

    (a)   the action is triggered when you click the mouse button when the pointer is over the button.

    (b)   the action is triggered when you release the mouse button when the pointer is over the button. This is the default option.

(c)   the action is triggered when you release the mouse button when the pointer is not over the button.

(d)   the action is triggered when the mouse pointer passes over the button.

(e)   the action is triggered when the mouse pointer leaves the button.

(f)   the action is triggered when the mouse button is held down when the pointer is over the button, leaves the button then returns to the button.

(g)   the action is triggered when the mouse button is held down over the button then the pointer leaves the button.

(h)   the action is triggered when the key specified in the corresponding text box is pressed.

② If necessary, add a new action that will run after the selected action and define its settings in the programming interface.

③ Once all the actions have been inserted and defined, save them in the movie.

⇨ *To test the button, use **Control - Enable Buttons** or* Ctrl Alt *B before playing the movie.*

D-Managing buttons

When you create a movie, Flash allows you to determine whether the buttons you create are enabled or not. Generally, buttons are not enabled when you are creating them. However, it can be useful to enable them because an enabled button reacts to events triggered by the mouse in the same way as it will when the movie is playing, which makes testing the button faster.

Buttons that contains movie clips cannot be tested in this way, you must test the movie itself.

Enabling or disabling buttons

▒ Tick the **Enable Buttons** option in the **Control** menu or press Ctrl Alt **B**.

▒ Deactivate the **Enable Buttons** option in the **Control** menu or press Ctrl Alt **B** to disable buttons.

Selecting and editing enabled buttons

▒ Activate the **Arrow** tool and draw a rectangle around the button concerned to select it.

▒ To move the button, use the arrow keys on the keyboard.

▒ To edit the button, use **Modify - Instance** to open the **Instance Properties** dialog box and make your changes.

Testing an interactive button that does not contain a movie clip

▓ Select the button concerned using the **Arrow tool** [arrow cursor icon].

▓ Tick the **Enable Buttons** option in the **Control** menu or press Ctrl Alt **B**.

▓ Carry out the test (click, drag, hold down the mouse button and so forth).

6.1 Tests

A- Overview

In order to check that all the components of your movie work correctly, you must carry out some tests. You should test all the scenes individually, then the entire movie.

While Flash can play a movie from the working file (.fla) in the creation environment, most features in an interactive movie will not work if the movie has not been exported in its final format (Shockwave - .swf).

The **Control** menu commands allow Flash to export the current movie (.fla) as a Flash movie (.swf), and play the movie immediately in a new window. A movie exported in this way in its final format uses the options defined in the **Publish Settings** dialog box (see 6.2 - B - Defining the publish settings).

(see 6.2 - B - Defining the publish settings)

After you test a movie, this is what you can see:

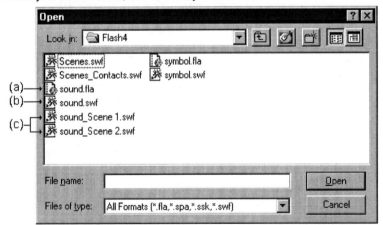

(a) working file contains the complete movie: its name is the name of the movie with the extension .fla.

(b) Shockwave file generated automatically by Flash when you first test the complete movie: its name consists of the name of the movie followed by .swf.

(c) Shockwave file generated automatically by Flash when you first test this scene of the movie. Its name includes the name of the movie and the scene followed by .swf. Notice that the Shockwave files are in the same folder as the working files.

B-Testing a scene

▦ Open the working file that contains the scene you want to test using the **Open** command in the **File** menu.

▦ Activate the scene concerned by selecting it from the **View - Goto** menu.

▦ **Control - Test Scene** or Ctrl Alt Enter

Flash exports the scene to a specific .swf file whose name is the name of the movie followed by the name of the scene. This file is created in the same folder as the .fla file, and is opened in a new window and played using Flash Player.

▦ To stop a movie, close the .swf file using the **Close** command in the **File** menu.

⇨ *When a scene has already been tested, you can retest it by opening the export file (for example: movie_scene1.swf) using* **File - Open**.

C-Testing a movie

▦ To test all the interactive features and animations in a movie, open the .fla working file concerned using **File - Open**.

▦ **Control - Test Movie** or Ctrl Enter

Flash exports the movie into a new .swf file in the same folder as the .fla file then opens this new file in a new window and plays it using Flash Player.

▦ To stop a movie, close the .swf file using the **Close** command from the **File** menu.

D-Testing the downloading of a scene or movie

It is important to simulate the playing of your movie under online conditions. This means that you have an idea of how quickly the movie plays in a browser.

To simulate the download speed, Flash 4 takes the modem speed Into account but also the standard performance of the Internet. Thus, while a 28.8 Kbps modem can theoretically download data at 3.5 Kb/sec, if you active the command Control - 28.8, Flash will use a more realistic debit of 2.3 Kb/sec.

▒ Before testing the downloading of a scene or movie, make sure that the **Publish Settings** are correct.

▒ Use **Control - Test Scene** or **Control - Test Movie**, depending on the case.

Flash 4 exports the scene or movie as a .swf file and opens it in a new window (see 6.1 - B - Testing a scene or C - Testing a movie).

▒ Open the **Control** menu.

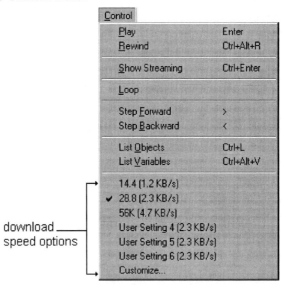

download speed options

▒ Activate the download speed you want or click the **Customize** option to define your own values.

▒ To carry out a new test, use **Control - Rewind** or [Ctrl][Alt] **R** then **Control - Play** or [Enter].

The movie or scene is now tested using the newly-defined download speed.

▒ Retest with other speeds if necessary.

▒ Close the movie file (.swf) using **File - Close** or [Ctrl] **W**.

E- Using the publish preview

*The principle of the **Publish Preview** command is to export the file type selected in the dialog box that corresponds to this command, and to open it in your computer's default browser.*

▓ To preview a file using Flash's **Publish Preview** command, first define the export settings in the **Publish Settings** dialog box (see 6.2 - B - Defining the publish settings).

▓ **File - Publish Preview**

choose the file format
you want to preview

*Taking the **Publish Settings** into account, Flash generates a file following the chosen type and inserts it in the same folder as the movie itself. You will keep this file as long as it is not replaced or deleted.*

⇨ *The* F12 *key exports and previews the movie using the **Default** format.*

F- Making a backup of a movie

▓ Before you publish a movie, make backups of your Flash files. You should create a folder just for this purpose on your disk and place in it all the graphics and sounds from the movie. You should also place the final version of the movie in this folder. This data will be indispensable if you want to edit a published movie.

6.2 Exporting and publishing

A-General principles

When you open a Flash Player in a browser, you open an HTML document, which activates the Flash Player and plays the movie.

If a browser is to be able to read a Flash movie, it must have the Flash Player. Recent browsers have this application, provided all their components are installed. Viewers of your movie can find out whether or not they have the Flash Player on their system with a simple test. For this, Flash includes the **Detect** file in the application's installation folder (by default: \Program Files\Macromedia\Flash 4\Sample Pages\Detect Flash 4). This file will detect whether the current version of the Player is available, and if it is not a link to the Macromedia site is given, allowing the user to download the Player. Go ahead and integrate this file into your movie.

The principle file format for publishing Flash data is Flash Player format (or Shockwave Flash-.swf). This is the only format that supports all of Flash's interactive features.

There are different techiques for reading a Flash Player movie:
- in Internet browsers, such as Netscape and Internet Explorer, which have Flash Player.
- with Flash Xtra in Director and Authorware.
- with the ActiveX Flash control in Microsoft Office and other ActiveX hosts.
- as part of a QuickTime movie.
- as an autonomous movie, called Projector.

Flash 4

Export file formats

▦ As mentioned previously, the main format for exported movies is Shockwave (.swf), but Flash can also export independent images in a number of formats: EPS, GIF, JPEG, PNG, BMP, SPL, MOV, WMF, WAV, PICT, QuickTime and AVI.

Flash commands: Publish or Export

▦ The **Publish** command has the particularity of creating all the files your Web Flash application needs in one go and with one command. In fact, not only does this command create the Flash Player (.swf) file, but also the graphic files using the different available formats as substitute images (see Publish settings) and an HTML document that has all the settings necessary for playing the movie.

▦ The **Export** command options are intended to provide files that can be edited in other applications. They enable you to export a file or a whole movie rapidly as a Flash Player file or as a series of bitmap images.

⇨ *Before exporting an audio movie, you can compress the sound files (see 4.6 - G - Compressing a sound file).*

B-Defining the publish settings

▦ **File - Publish Settings** or ⌃Ctrl ⇧Shift F12

The formats to create

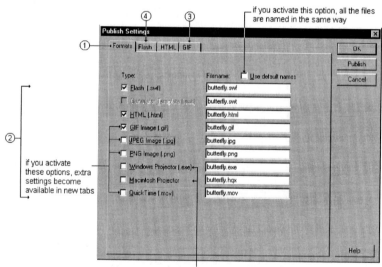

if you activate this option, all the files are named in the same way

if you activate these options, extra settings become available in new tabs

these options create a file containing Flash Player that can be used on CDs and other supports

① Activate this tab.

② Choose the file formats that should be created with the **Publish** command. For some formats, Flash offers extra settings in a new tab. All the formats cannot be created on some computers, and the QuickTime format can only be created if an adapted Player is installed.

③ Click the tab that corresponds to the format you have chosen to define its publication settings (in the example the format is GIF).

④ Activate this tab to define Flash's publication settings.

⇨ *For each active image format, Flash 4 automatically creates the HTML code necessary to read the file in a specific file.*

Flash publish settings

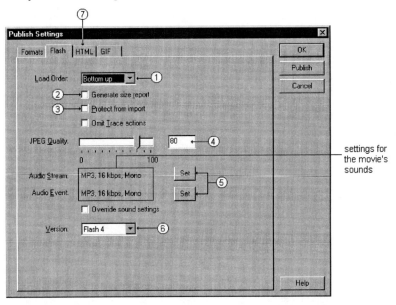

settings for
the movie's
sounds

① Define the order in which the layers should load in the first frame using one of these options. You should choose the **Top down** option for an Internet connection.

② Activate this option to create a text (.txt) file containing the dimensions of and data about the Flash file objects.

③ Activate this option to protect your movie against use by an unauthorised person: the .swf file will not be able to be re-imported into Flash 4.

④ This ruler defines the JPEG compression of bitmap images. The lower the file quality, the smaller the files are. 100 corresponds to the best quality. Drag the cursor along the ruler to define the JPEG quality, or type a value in the corresponding text box.

⑤ Click these buttons to change the compression settings if they have not been defined separately in the audio properties.

⑥ Make sure the movie can only be played by the specified Player. The Flash 4 Player can also create Flash 3 and older formats. However, a Flash 2 Player cannot read Flash 4 format.

⑦ Activate this tab to define the HTML file settings, if necessary.

HTML publish settings

A browser shows a Flash movie on the Web by reading the correspon-
ding HTML files. A Flash movie's HTML file loads the movie and plays it.
The HTML settings defined in this tab are inserted in a template docu-
ment.

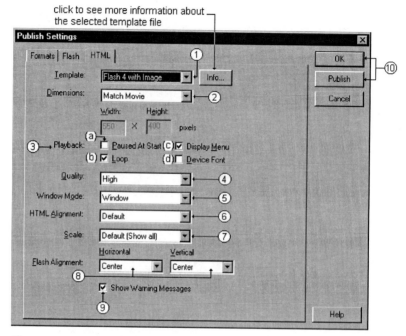

① Open this list of template files in the HTML folder in the Flash 4 installation folder and select the one you want to use. Some basic templates only show the movie in the browser, and other more elaborate
templates contain, notably, code that can detect the browser. If you do
not choose a template, Flash uses the default template Default.htm.
Flash saves the edited template under the Flash movie's name, followed by the template extension .asp. If, for example, you have chosen
to use the template Template.asp with the movie Project.swf, the final
file will be called Project.asp.

② Open this list to define the WIDTH and HEIGHT of the OBJECT and
EMBED tags. These tags insert the movie into the HTML file. Choose
one of the options:

Match Movie to define the dimensions with reference to those of
the movie.

Pixels to enter the number of pixels in the **Width** and
Height boxes.

| **Percent** | to define the dimensions of the movie according to the size of the browser window. Enter the percentages you want in the **Width** and **Height** boxes. |

③ Activate the appropriate options to define the values for the settings LOOP, PLAY, MENU and DEVICE FONT of the OBJECT and EMBED tags.

(a)	this option sets the PLAY parameter to FALSE. The movie does not play automatically once it is loaded. This option is generally defined as TRUE, so that the movie will start to play automatically once it is loaded.
(b)	this option sets the LOOP parameter to TRUE. The movie repeats itself.
(c)	this option sets the MENU parameter to TRUE. If it is deactivated the movie player does not have a context menu with which to control the movie. Only information about the Player is displayed.
(d)	this option sets the DEVICE FONT parameter to TRUE, and replaces the fonts in the movie that are not available on the user's computer with Flash equivalents.

④ Define the QUALITY parameter of the OBJECT and EMBED tags and specify the antialiasing (anti-pixelisation) level by choosing one of these options:

Low	to give priority to play-speed to the detriment of appearance. The antialiasing option is never used with this option.
Auto Low	to prioritise speed, but improve the appearance whenever possible.
Auto High	to prioritise the appearance when necessary, to the detriment of speed.
High	to prefer the appearance rather than the speed. In this case, antialiasing is always used.
Best	to produce the best display quality and ignore the play-speed.

⑤ Choose the WMODE settings for the OBJECT tag. You can now benefit from the advantages of transparent movies, absolute positioning and layering capabilities of Internet Explorer 4.0 or higher. This feature is not supported by other browsers.

⑥ Choose the ALIGN settings for the OBJECT, IMG and EMBED tags in order to define the position of the Flash movie window in the browser window.

⑦ Choose the SCALE value for the OBJECT and EMBED tags so that you can define the position of the movie inside the frame indicated in the **Width** and **Height** boxes:

| **Default** | the whole movie is visible in the defined area, and the original dimensions of the movie are preserved. |
| **No border** | resizes the movie so that it fills the defined area, keeping the original proportions of the movie. |

TESTING/PUBLISHING/EXPORTING

Exact fit   the whole movie is visible in the defined area, but its original proportions are not necessarily preserved.

⑧ Set the SALIGN parameter for the OBJECT and EMBED tags. The values of the **Horizontal** and **Vertical** boxes define the position of the movie in its window.

⑨ If this option is active, Flash 4 displays an error message if you choose contradictory settings. For example, if a template contains code that refers to a replacement image that has not been defined.

⑩ Once you have defined all the settings, click the **OK** button to confirm them and close the dialog box, or click **Publish** to go ahead and publish the files using the different formats you have just defined.

C-Publishing a movie

▓ Open the movie concerned.

▓ **File - Publish Settings** or `Ctrl` `⇧ Shift` `F12`, and define the settings you require (see 6.2 - B - Defining the publish settings).

▓ Click **Publish**.

⇨ *If you do not want to change any of the settings, you can use File - Publish or* `⇧ Shift` `F12`.

D-Editing or updating a published movie

▓ To edit or update a Flash Player movie created with the **Publish** command, open the original Flash movie.

▓ Make the necessary changes.

▓ Use the **Publish** command again.

E-Exporting an image or movie

▓ To export an image from the current movie, select the image concerned. If you want to export the whole movie, do not select anything.

▓ Use **File - Export Movie** or **File - Export Image**, depending on the case.

in this example, an image is being exported

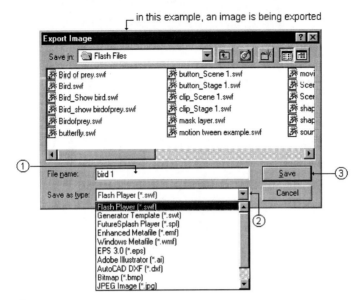

① Type the name of the output file.

② Open this list and choose the export file type for a picture, or the **Format** for a movie.

③ Confirm the exportation.

*If the selected format requires more information, an **Export** dialog box opens.*

▓ In this case, define the exportation options for the chosen format and confirm with **OK**.

⇨ *The export options for a Flash movie are the same as those defined in* ***Publish Settings***.

Windows Shortcut Keys

File

New	`Ctrl` N
Open	`Ctrl` O
Open as Library	`Ctrl` `⇧ Shift` O
Close	`Ctrl` W
Save	`Ctrl` S
Save as	`Ctrl` `⇧ Shift` S
Import	`Ctrl` R
Export movie	`Ctrl` `Alt` `⇧ Shift` S
Print	`Ctrl` P
Quit	`Ctrl` Q

Edit

Undo	`Ctrl` Z
Redo	`Ctrl` Y
Cut	`Ctrl` X
Copy	`Ctrl` C
Paste	`Ctrl` V
Paste in place	`Ctrl` `⇧ Shift` V
Clear	`Del`
Duplicate	`Ctrl` D
Select all	`Ctrl` A
Deselect all	`Ctrl` `⇧ Shift` A
Copy frames	`Ctrl` `Alt` C
Paste frames	`Ctrl` `Alt` V
Edit symbols	`Ctrl` E

View

100%	`Ctrl` 1
Show frame	`Ctrl` 2
Show all	`Ctrl` 3
Outlines	`Ctrl` `Alt` `⇧ Shift` O
Fast	`Ctrl` `Alt` `⇧ Shift` F
Antialias	`Ctrl` `Alt` `⇧ Shift` A
Antialias text	`Ctrl` `Alt` `⇧ Shift` T
Timeline	`Ctrl` `Alt` T
Work area	`Ctrl` `⇧ Shift` W

Rulers	`Ctrl` `Alt` `⇧ Shift`	**R**
Grids	`Ctrl` `Alt` `⇧ Shift`	**G**
Snap	`Ctrl` `Alt`	**G**
Show shape hints	`Ctrl` `Alt`	**H**

Go To

First	`Home`
Previous	`Pg Up`
Next	`Pg Dn`
Last	`End`

Insert

Convert to symbol	`F 8`
Frame	`F 5`
Delete frame	`⇧ Shift` `F 5`
Keyframe	`F 6`
Blank keyframe	`F 7`
Clear keyframe	`⇧ Shift` `F 6`

Modify

Instance	`Ctrl` **I**
Frame	`Ctrl` **F**
Movie	`Ctrl` **M**
Font	`Ctrl` **T**
Paragraph	`Ctrl` `⇧ Shift` **T**
Align	`Ctrl` **K**
Group	`Ctrl` **G**
Ungroup	`Ctrl` `⇧ Shift` **G**
Break Apart	`Ctrl` **B**

Style

Plain	`Ctrl` `⇧ Shift` **P**
Bold	`Ctrl` `⇧ Shift` **B**
Italic	`Ctrl` `⇧ Shift` **I**
Align left	`Ctrl` `⇧ Shift` **L**
Align centre	`Ctrl` `⇧ Shift` **C**
Align right	`Ctrl` `⇧ Shift` **R**
Justify	`Ctrl` `⇧ Shift` **J**

SHORTCUT KEYS

Kerning

Narrower   `Ctrl` `Alt` `←`

Wider   `Ctrl` `Alt` `→`

Reset   `Ctrl` `Alt` `↑`

Transform

Scale and rotate   `Ctrl` `Alt` S

Remove transform   `Ctrl` `⇧ Shift` Z

Add shape hint   `Ctrl` H

Arrange

Bring to front   `Ctrl` `⇧ Shift` `↑`

Move ahead   `Ctrl` `↑`

Move behind   `Ctrl` `↓`

Send to back   `Ctrl` `⇧ Shift` `↓`

Lock   `Ctrl` `Alt` L

Unlock all   `Ctrl` `Alt` `⇧ Shift` L

Curves

Optimise   `Ctrl` `Alt` `⇧ Shift` C

Control

Play   `Enter`

Rewind   `Ctrl` `Alt` R

Step forward   >

Step backward   <

Test movie   `Ctrl` `Enter`

Test scene   `Ctrl` `Alt` `Enter`

Enable frame actions   `Ctrl` `Alt` A

Enable buttons   `Ctrl` `Alt` B

Mute sounds   `Ctrl` `Alt` M

Window

New window   `Ctrl` `Alt` N

Inspector   `Ctrl` `Alt` I

Library   `Ctrl` L

Macintosh Shortcut Keys

File

New	⌘		N
Open	⌘		O
Open as Library	⌘	⇧ Shift	O
Close	⌘		W
Save	⌘		S
Save as	⌘	⇧ Shift	S
Import	⌘		R
Export movie	⌘	⇧ Shift ⌥	S
Print	⌘		P
Quit	⌘		Q

Edit

Undo	⌘		Z
Redo	⌘		Y
Cut	⌘		X
Copy	⌘		C
Paste	⌘		V
Paste in place	⌘	⇧ Shift	V
Clear	Del		
Duplicate	⌘		D
Select all	⌘		A
Deselect all	⌘	⇧ Shift	A
Copy frames	⌘	⌥	C
Paste frames	⌘	⌥	V
Edit symbols	⌘		E

View

100%	⌘		1
Show frame	⌘		2
Show all	⌘		3
Outlines	⇧ Shift ⌥ ⌘		O
Fast	⇧ Shift ⌥ ⌘		F
Antialias	⇧ Shift ⌥ ⌘		A
Antialias text	⇧ Shift ⌥ ⌘		T
Timeline	⌘ ⌥		T
Work area	⌘ ⇧ Shift		W

SHORTCUT KEYS

Rules	⌘	⌥	⇧ Shift R
Grid	⌘	⌥	⇧ Shift G
Snap	⌘	⌥	G
Show shape hints	⌘	⌥	H

Go To

First	⤒
Previous	Pg Up
Next	Pg Dn
Last	⤓

Insert

Convert to symbol	F8
Frame	F5
Delete frame	⇧ Shift F5
Keyframe	F6
Blank keyframe	F7
Clear keyframe	⇧ Shift F6

Modify

Instance	⌘ I
Frame	⌘ F
Movie	⌘ M
Font	⌘ T
Paragraph	⌘ ⇧ Shift T
Align	⌘ K
Group	⌘ G
Ungroup	⌘ ⇧ Shift G
Break appart	⌘ B

Style

Plain	⌘ ⇧ Shift P
Bold	⌘ ⇧ Shift B
Italic	⌘ ⇧ Shift I
Align left	⌘ ⇧ Shift L
Align centre	⌘ ⇧ Shift C
Align right	⌘ ⇧ Shift R
Justify	⌘ ⇧ Shift J

Kerning

Narrower	⌘ ⌥ ←

Wider	⌘ ⌥ →
Reset	⌘ ⌥ ↑

Transform
Scale and rotate	⌘ ⌥ S
Remove transform	⌘ ⇧ Shift Z
Add shape hint	⌘ H

Arrange
Bring to front	⌘ ⇧ Shift ↑
Move ahead	⌘ ↑
Move behind	⌘ ↓
Send to back	⌘ ⇧ Shift ↓
Lock	⌘ ⌥ L
Unlock all	⌘ ⌥ ⇧ Shift L

Curves
Optimise	⌘ ⌥ ⇧ Shift C

Control
Play	↵
Rewind	⌘ ⌥ R
Step forward	>
Step backward	<
Test movie	⌘ ↵
Test scene	⌘ ⌥ ↵
Enable frame actions	⌘ ⌥ A
Enable buttons	⌘ ⌥ B
Mute sounds	⌘ ⌥ M

Window
New window	⌘ ⌥ N
Inspectors	⌘ ⌥ I
Library	⌘ L

Some sites that use Flash

http://www.thesimpsons.com
http://www.landrover.co.uk
http://www.sleepyhollowmovie.com
http://www.svjeans.com
http://www.hover.co.uk
http://www.coke.com
http://www.greets.com

You can find links to more sites at Macromedia's site:
http://www.macromedia.com/software/flash/gallery/collection

A

B

C

D

E

F

G

M

O

T

U

V

W

Z

INDEX BY SUBJECT